Collins | English for Exams

Cambridge English Qualifications

A2 Key
for Schools

8 practice tests

Published by Collins
An imprint of HarperCollins Publishers
Westerhill Road
Bishopbriggs
Glasgow
G64 2QT

HarperCollins Publishers
Macken House
39/40 Mayor Street Upper
Dublin 1
D01 C9W8
Ireland

First edition 2020

10 9

© HarperCollins Publishers 2020

ISBN 978-0-00-836755-8

If you would like to comment on any aspect of this book, please contact us at the given address or online. E-mail: collins.elt@harpercollins.co.uk

Authors: Sarah Jane Lewis, Patrick McMahon
Series editor: Celia Wigley
For the Publisher: Lisa Todd and Sheena Shanks
Editor: Anastasia Vassilatou
Typesetter: Jouve, India
Illustrations: Jouve, India
Photographs p40: Xinhua/Alamy Stock Photo, p112: ZUMA Press, Inc./Alamy Stock Photo
All other photographs: Shutterstock.com
Printer: Printed and bound by Ashford Colour Press Ltd.
Audio recorded and produced by ID Audio, London
Cover designer: Gordon McGilp
Cover illustration: Maria Herbert-Liew
Sample Answer sheets (pages 196–9): Reproduced with permission of Cambridge Assessment English © UCLES 2019

About the authors

Sarah Jane Lewis is an experienced writer and editor of primary and secondary course material with over 10 years' experience in the education publishing sector, working with organisations across Europe, Asia and North and South America. As well as working as a teacher of academic and general English to young learners, teens and adults in the UK and Greece, she also has experience in preparing candidates for Cambridge English exams and has a special interest in young learners and assessment. She is the author of a variety of engaging books and materials for young learners and young adults.

Patrick McMahon is a university lecturer, teacher trainer, materials writer and academic. He has taught English in universities, colleges, secondary schools and language schools in the UK, mainland Europe, Asia and the Middle East. He has written a broad range of materials for publishers and specialises in English for Academic Purposes.

MIX
Paper | Supporting responsible forestry
FSC
www.fsc.org   FSC™ C007454

This book contains FSC™ certified paper and other controlled sources to ensure responsible forest management.

For more information visit: www.harpercollins.co.uk/green

Contents

How to use this book

Who is this book for?

This book will help you to prepare for the *Cambridge Assessment English A2 Key for Schools* exam. The exam is also known as the *KET for Schools* exam. The exam was updated for 2020 and this book was written for the new exam. This book will be useful if you are preparing for the exam for the first time or taking it again. The book has been designed so that you can use it to study on your own, however, you can also use it if you are preparing for the *A2 Key for Schools* exam in a class.

The book contains:

- **Tips for success** – important advice to help you to do well in the exam
- **About A2 Key for Schools** – a guide to the exam
- **How to prepare for the test** – advice to help you to succeed in each part
- **Practice tests** – eight complete practice tests
- **Mini-dictionary** – definitions of the more difficult words from the practice tests
- **Audio scripts** – the texts of what you hear in the Listening and Speaking parts
- **Sample answer sheets** – make sure you know what the answer sheets look like
- **Answer key** – the answers for Reading and Listening
- **Model answers** – examples of good answers for the Writing and Speaking parts
- **Speaking: Additional practice by topic** – more sample questions to help you prepare for the Speaking test
- **Audio** – all the recordings for the practice tests as well as model answers for Speaking are available online at collins.co.uk/eltresources

Tips for success

- **Start studying early** – The more you practise, the better your English will become. Give yourself at least two months to revise and complete all the practice tests in this book. Spend at least one hour a day studying.
- **Time yourself** when you do the practice tests. This will help you to feel more confident when you do the real exam.
- **Do every part** of each practice test. Don't be afraid to make notes in the book. For example, writing down the meaning of words you don't know on the page itself will help you to remember them later on.

Using the book for self-study

If you haven't studied for the *A2 Key for Schools* exam before, it is a good idea to do all the tests in this book in order. If you have a teacher or friend who can help you with your speaking and writing, that would be very useful. It is also a good idea to meet up with other students who are preparing for the exam or who want to improve their English. Having a study partner will help you to stay motivated. You can also help each other with areas of English you might find difficult.

Begin preparing for the *A2 Key for Schools* exam by getting to know the different parts of the exam, what each part tests and how many marks there are for each part. Use the information in the **About A2 Key for Schools** section to find out all you can. You can also download the *A2 Key for Schools Handbook* from the Cambridge Assessment English website for more details.

You need to know how to prepare for each of the parts of the exam in the best way possible. The **How to prepare for the test** section in this book will be useful. Try to follow the advice as it will help you to develop the skills you need.

In the practice tests in this book, you will see certain words highlighted in grey. These are the more difficult words and you can find definitions of these in the **Mini-dictionary** at the back of the book. The definitions are from *Collins COBUILD* dictionaries. It's a good idea to download the *Cambridge A2*

Key Vocabulary List from the Cambridge Assessment English website. This is a list of words that you should understand at A2 level and the list is the same if you're taking the *A2 Key* test or the *A2 Key for Schools* test. Look through the list and make a note of the words you don't know. Then look up their meaning in a dictionary. You could use the Collins online dictionary: www.collinsdictionary.com. Knowing these words will help you to do better in the exam. Search 'A2 Key Vocabulary List 2020'.

Preparing for the Writing and Speaking parts

When you are ready to try the practice tests, make sure you answer the questions in the Writing parts as well as the Speaking parts. You can only improve your skills by practising a lot. Practise writing to a time limit. If you find this difficult at first, start by writing a very good answer of the correct length without worrying about time. Then try to complete your writing faster until you can write a good answer within the time limit. Learn to estimate the number of words you have written without counting them. Study the model answers at the back of the book. This will give you a clear idea of the standard your answers need to be. Don't try to memorise emails, notes or stories for the Writing part or answers to the questions in the Speaking part. If you work your way through the book, you should develop the skills and language you need to give good answers in the real exam.

The Speaking part in this book has accompanying audio so that you can practise answering the examiner's questions. You will be Candidate B, so if you hear the examiner ask Candidate B a question, this means you should answer by pausing the audio on your computer and answering the question. In Part 2 of the Speaking test, you are expected to have a conversation with Candidate A. Again, you will be Candidate B and will respond to Candidate A's statements or questions. This experience will not be 100% authentic as Candidate A cannot respond to your statements or questions, however, this book and the audio have been designed to give you an excellent opportunity to practise answering questions through the eight practice tests. Once you have finished the Speaking part, you can listen to the model answers for Candidate B that have been provided for you. Another option is that you record your answers and then compare these with the model answers.

Please note that there are two versions of the Speaking Test audio:

* The first version contains the pauses for you to practise answering the questions in the Speaking tests. This is when you have to answer the questions for Candidate B. The scripts for this audio can be found from page 167 onwards in your book. For example, you'll see on page 169 that Test 1 Speaking audio track is labelled 'Track 06'. Look for Track 06 when you search for the audio online.

* The second version of the audio contains the Model Answers for the Speaking tests. These are for you to listen to, to see how a good student might answer the questions in the Speaking test. The scripts for this audio can be found from page 207 onwards in your book. You'll see that these audio files are labelled with an 'a' at the end, for example Track 06a, etc. Look for Track 06a when you search for the audio online.

At the back of the book you'll find more sample questions for the Speaking test. These provide another opportunity to practise answering questions that an examiner might ask you. There are 16 topics and all the questions have been recorded. Try answering these questions as fully as possible. Don't just give a 'yes/no' answer but try to give a reason or an example in your answer.

Finally, read as much as possible in English; this is the best way to learn new vocabulary and improve your English.

About A2 Key for Schools

The *Cambridge A2 Key for Schools* exam is a pre-intermediate-level English exam delivered by Cambridge Assessment English. It is for school students who need to show that they can deal with everyday English at a pre-intermediate level. In other words, you have to be able to:

- understand simple written information such as signs and notes
- write in simple English on everyday subjects
- show you can follow and understand a range of spoken materials such as announcements when people speak reasonably slowly
- show you can take part in different types of interactions using simple spoken English.

The exam is one of several offered by Cambridge Assessment English at different levels. The table below shows how *A2 Key for Schools* fits into the Cambridge English Qualifications. The level of this exam is described as being at A2 on the Common European Framework of Reference (CEFR).

	CEFR	Cambridge English Scale	Cambridge qualification
Proficient user	C2	200–230	C2 Proficiency
	C1	180–199	C1 Advanced
Independent user	B2	160–179	B2 First for Schools
	B1	140–159	B1 Preliminary for Schools
Basic user	A2	120–139	A2 Key for Schools
	A1	100–119	A1 Movers
	Pre-A1	80–99	Pre A1 Starters

The *A2 Key for Schools* qualification is for school students and it is an ideal first exam for those new to learning English and it gives learners confidence to study for higher Cambridge English Qualifications. Cambridge Assessment English also offers an *A2 Key* qualification. Both tests follow the same format and the candidates are tested in the same skills. However, the content of the exam is a bit different. The *A2 Key for Schools* is for candidates who are at school and is designed to suit the interests and experiences of school-age candidates. The *A2 Key* exam is for older students studying general English or those in higher education. If you are an adult learner, it would be better for you to take the *A2 Key* qualification and use the *Collins Practice Tests for A2 Key* to prepare for the exam.

There are three papers (or tests) in **A2 Key for Schools**:

- Paper 1: Reading and Writing (1 hour)
- Paper 2: Listening (approximately 30 minutes)
- Paper 3: Speaking (8–10 minutes)

Timetabling
You usually take the Reading and Writing test and the Listening test on the same day. The Speaking test may take place on a different day and it may be before or after the other tests. If you are studying on your own, you should contact your exam centre for dates. The exam is paper based. You can also take the exam on computer in some countries. For more information, see: https://www.cambridge-exams.ch/exams/CB_exams.php.

Paper/Test 1 Reading and Writing (1 hour)

Candidates need to be able to understand simple written information, such as signs and newspapers, and produce simple written English.

The **Reading and Writing** test has seven parts. Reading parts 1–5 have 30 questions and there is one mark for each question. Writing parts 6 and 7 have only one question each. Students should spend about 40 minutes on the Reading parts and about 20 minutes on the Writing parts of this test.

The Reading section has five parts.

Part 1 has six short emails, notices, signs or text messages. There are three sentences next to each one. You have to choose which sentence matches the meaning of the email, notice, sign or text message. (Total marks: 6)

Part 2 has seven questions and three short texts on the same topic. You have to match each question to one of the texts. (Total marks: 7)

Part 3 has a longer text, for example, a simplified newspaper or magazine article. There are five multiple-choice questions with three options, A, B and C. (Total marks: 5)

Part 4 has a short text with six numbered spaces. You decide which of the three words provided belongs in each gap. (Total marks: 6)

Part 5 has a short text with six gaps. You have to fill in six gaps in a text or texts using single words. (Total marks: 6)

The Writing section has two parts: Parts 6 and 7 of the Reading and Writing test.

In **Part 6** you write a short email or note. This should be 25 words or more. (Total marks: 15)

In **Part 7** you write a short story using picture prompts. This should be 35 words based on three picture prompts. (Total marks: 15)

In each part, marks are awarded in the following ways:
- five marks if you include all the necessary information
- five marks if you organise your message so a reader can follow it easily
- five marks if you use a good range of grammar structures and vocabulary.

Paper/Test 2 Listening (30 minutes)

Candidates need to show they can follow and understand a range of spoken materials, such as announcements, when people speak reasonably slowly.

The Listening test has five parts and there are 25 questions in total.

Part 1 has five short dialogues, for example, conversations at home or in a shop, and five questions. For each question, you have to listen and choose the correct answer from three options: A, B or C. The options are pictures. (Total marks: 5)

Part 2 has a longer text. You listen and write the missing information (prices, times, telephone numbers) in the gaps. You should write only one word, or a number, or a date, or a time for your answer. (Total marks: 5)

Part 3 has a longer informal conversation. You listen and choose the correct answer to a question from three options: A, B or C. The questions include opinions and attitudes of the speaker. (Total marks: 5)

Part 4 has five short conversations. You listen and choose the best answer from the three options: A, B or C. (Total marks: 5)

Part 5 has a longer conversation between two people who know each other. You match each of five items in the first list with five of the eight items in the second list. (Total marks: 5)

Paper/Test 3 Speaking (8–10 minutes)

Candidates take the Speaking test with another candidate or in a group of three. You are tested on your ability to take part in different types of interaction: with the examiner, with the other candidate and by yourself.

The Speaking test has two parts.

In **Part 1** the examiner asks you some questions about your name, where you live, your daily life, etc. and then the examiner asks you a longer 'Tell me something about ...' question. You respond to the examiner. (Time: 3–4 minutes)

In **Part 2**, the examiner gives you five pictures on a particular topic, e.g. hobbies. You talk together with the other candidate and discuss the activities, things or places in the pictures. After you have spoken for 1–2 minutes, the examiner continues the conversation by asking you questions related to the pictures. Then the examiner asks you two more questions on the same topic. (Time: 4–6 minutes)

Marks and results

After the exam, all candidates receive a Statement of Results. Candidates whose performance ranges between CEFR Levels A1 and B1 (Cambridge English Scale scores of 100–150) also receive a certificate.

The Statement of Results shows the candidate's:

- score on the Cambridge English Scale for their performance in each of the four language skills (reading, writing, listening and speaking).
- score on the Cambridge English Scale for their overall performance in the exam. This overall score is the average of their scores for the four skills.
- grade – this is based on the candidate's overall score.
- level on the CEFR – this is also based on the overall score.

The certificate shows the candidate's:

- score on the Cambridge English Scale for each of the four skills.
- overall score on the Cambridge English Scale.
- grade.
- level on the CEFR.
- level on the UK National Qualifications Framework (NQF).

For *A2 Key for Schools*, the following scores will be used to report results:

Cambridge English Scale Score	Grade	CEFR Level
140–150	A	B1
133–139	B	A2
120–132	C	A2
100–119	Level A1	A1

Grade A: Cambridge English Scale scores of 140–150

Candidates sometimes show ability beyond Level A2. If a candidate achieves a Grade A in their exam, they will receive the *Key English Test for Schools* certificate stating that they demonstrated ability at Level B1.

Grades B and Grade C: Cambridge English Scale scores of 120–139

If a candidate achieves a Grade B or Grade C in their exam, they will receive the *Key English Test for Schools* certificate at Level A2.

CEFR Level A1: Cambridge English Scale scores of 100–119

If a candidate's performance is below Level A2, but falls within Level A1, they will receive a *Cambridge English* certificate stating that they demonstrated ability at Level A1.

Scores between 100 and 119 are also reported on your Statement of Results, but you will not receive a *Key English Test for Schools* certificate.

For more information on how the exam is marked, go to: http://www.cambridgeenglish.org

Working through the practice tests in this book will improve your exam skills, help you with timing for the exam, give you confidence and help you get a better result in the exam.

Good luck!

How to prepare for the test

The practice tests in this book will help you to get ready for the test. They will give you a clear understanding of the types of questions you have to answer so you know exactly what the test will be like. This means there will be no surprises for you on the day of the test. The *A2 Key for Schools* test is a test of your general English language skills. This means that you should continue to work hard to improve your general level of English to prepare for the test. This section of the book gives you suggestions for improving your general level of English and on how to prepare for the test itself.

Improving your general level of English

You need to do activities which will improve the four skills of reading, writing, listening and speaking as well as improving your knowledge of grammar and vocabulary. Here are some suggestions on how to develop these areas of your English.

Developing your reading skills

The best way to develop your reading skills is to read as much as you can. Reading a lot will improve all areas of your English as well as your reading skills. You should:

- learn about different types of reading: reading for enjoyment and reading for learning. Sometimes when you read you should relax, not worry too much about the new words and just try to enjoy it. But other times when you are reading you should work hard and look at the new words and the grammar. Think about these different types of reading so that you know which type of reading you are doing each time. Both types of reading will improve your general level of English. Reading for enjoyment will be good for your fluency. Reading for learning will be good for your vocabulary and grammar.

- decide how much time you can spend reading every day and make a reading schedule. Make a note of what you read so you can look back and see what you have done. This will help to keep you on track, and it will help you to see your progress.

- read the news and magazine articles in English. Don't worry about understanding every word you see. Read for general information and only look up new words which you think are important. There are some news websites which are made for English-language students which you can find easily on the Internet. Think of topics that you like, such as sport, or fashion, and try to read articles on those topics. It will be easier to read articles on topics that you are interested in than on topics you are not interested in. The BBC Learning English website is a good place to start and it has articles for different levels of English learners: http://www.bbc.co.uk/learningenglish/english/.

- read 'English readers', which are real books made shorter and easier for English-language learners. They are carefully written for learners at all levels of English and contain lists of words to help you understand the story and learn new vocabulary. Collins publishes the Agatha Christie readers (murder mysteries) and Amazing People readers (stories about famous people) and you can order them easily online. Other publishers publish other readers. Look for readers on topics you are interested in, or for books that you know in your first language.

- practise reading texts quickly for general understanding and practise reading texts more slowly for detailed understanding. You can use reading exercises which are written for students at your level of English. They will practise a wide range of reading skills. These exercises are widely available in textbooks or online.

- always read and pay attention to signs and notices you see in English. Understanding these is important in the *A2 Key for Schools* test.

Improving your writing skills

As with reading, the best way to improve your writing skills is practice. This means writing regularly. Your teacher may give you writing tasks and give you feedback. You can also:

- keep your own English-language diary. At the end of each day spend five minutes writing freely about your day. Say what you did, who you saw and how you felt about what happened. You can keep your diary private, so when you write your diary don't worry too much about grammar or spelling mistakes. This way you will improve your English fluency and your confidence will grow.
- join together with friends to make a writing group. Sit down together and write. Share your writing with your friends and comment on each other's writing. Or you can send your writing to each other electronically.
- find a penpal and write to them regularly. Your school may be able to help with this. Or you can find websites that will match you to a penpal. Always take care when you communicate with people using the Internet. People might not be who they say they are so make sure you don't share anything private with them.
- read as much as you can. This will improve your writing skills too.
- do reading and writing activities together, for example, read a book and then write a short text saying why you enjoyed it.

Improving your listening skills

There are many opportunities for you to improve your listening skills using modern technology. You should:

- learn about different types of listening skills: listening for general understanding and listening for detail. When you practise listening for general understanding you will learn that you do not need to understand every single word or sentence you hear. This will help you relax when you are listening. When you listen for detail, try to understand every word by playing the audio over and over again and looking at the audio script.
- know that many of the 'English readers' mentioned in the Reading section above have audio recordings that you can listen to. Using these you can listen and read at the same time.
- listen to the news in English.
- listen to talks where you can read the speaker's words (subtitles). For example, TED.com has some talks for students. Choose a topic you are interested in and listen to the first two minutes of a talk. Try listening first of all without reading the subtitles. Then listen again with subtitles. Doing this regularly will improve your listening comprehension.
- watch films and television programmes in English, even if you don't understand everything.
- use listening exercises in textbooks or on the BBC Learning English website.

Improving your speaking skills

A2 Key for Schools tests how well you can communicate in English, so take every opportunity you can to speak as much as possible. Try not to worry too much about grammar and accuracy when you speak. Instead think about communicating and speaking as fluently as you can. You could:

- join an English Club at school or online, remembering to take care when communicating with people online.
- ask your family to agree to only speak English with each other for a short time, for example over dinner one night. Or agree with your friends to only talk English together for a short time.
- find songs you like in English and sing along with them.
- record yourself speaking and listen to it. You should know what your English sounds like to other people. If you can, compare it to examples of sentences from native speakers.
- speak to yourself out loud in English when you don't have someone else to speak to. This will help you to get used to saying the words.

Improving your grammar

A2 Key for Schools is a test of your general English language skills and it is not a grammar test. But you should improve your understanding of what is correct and what is not correct in English. You can:

- do grammar exercises. There are lots of grammar exercises at different levels in different textbooks or online. Make sure they are the right level and do not try to do too many. There is not a list of grammar items you need to learn for *A2 Key for Schools*, but the Cambridge Assessment website has activities you can use to improve your English at this level. The BBC Learning English website also has grammar practice activities.
- be systematic in your grammar practice and learning. Keep a note of topics that you have done exercises on and review the topics.
- read as much as you can because this will improve your grammar too.

Improving your vocabulary

You will learn some words without trying to learn them. But you will also have to study hard to learn a lot of new words that you need for *A2 Key for Schools*. You can:

- make your own dictionary. Keep a notebook that is just for new words and write down all the new words you learn in your notebook. Look through your notebook regularly to review your words.
- download the *A2 Key for Schools Vocabulary List* from the Cambridge Assessment website. Look through the list and study the words that you don't know.
- find an app to improve your vocabulary. There are many apps which you can download for free from the Internet. Make sure you choose one for your level of English, so the words are not too difficult or too easy.
- label items around your home and then you will review the words every time you see them. Usually you need to see a new word seven times before you can say that you know it and you can use it.
- learn about word building and word formation. You can build words using groups of letters at the beginning and the ends of words. When you learn a new word try to learn other forms of the word too and record the different forms in your notebook.
- practise your spelling of the new words you learn.
- read as much as you can because this will improve your vocabulary too.

Preparing for the test

It is very important that before you take the test, you understand exactly what you have do in each part of the test. Here are some suggestions for what to think about in each part of the test.

Reading

Reading **Parts 1, 2** and **3** are multiple-choice questions. Be careful with multiple-choice questions. Don't just choose an answer because it has the same words as the text. These answers are often not correct. You should:

- look for the meaning of the text in the multiple-choice answers. The correct answer has the same meaning as the text, but usually uses different words to describe it.
- cross out answers which you can see are wrong immediately to help you to focus.
- find exactly which part of the text gives you the answer to a question and circle it. Then check the answer options against the circled text. This will help you to find the answer.

In Reading **Part 1** you have to read six short messages and choose which of three sentences has the same meaning. You should:

- try to understand the context of the message. Ask yourself: Who wrote this? Whom did they write it to? And what is the relationship between the two people? Look what type of text it is to help you.
- read the three options (A, B and C) next to each text.
- cross out the options which you can see are wrong to help you to focus.
- look back at the longer texts and choose the answer with the same meaning.

In Reading **Part 2** you have to read three short texts about different people and find the answers to seven questions. The questions are usually to do with *who* does *what*. You should:

- read the three texts through quickly first to understand the general topic.
- look at the first question to find out which information you need to find in the text.
- read the three texts again quickly to find the information needed to answer the question and circle it, then read the information more carefully.
- continue checking the rest of the text for more information on the same question as there may be a better place in the text later which has a better match to the text.
- choose the best answer and move to the next question.

In Reading **Part 3** there is one longer text to read. It is usually in the style of an article from a magazine or a newspaper. There are five multiple-choice questions to answer. Each answer has three options. You should:

- first read the text quickly to understand its general meaning and then read it again more slowly for more detail.
- look at the first question and find the relevant part of the text for that question, circle it and study it carefully.
- look back at the options and choose the option with the same meaning, and then check that the other options are wrong.
- then move on to the next question.

In Reading **Part 4** you have to fill in the gaps in a text. There are six gaps and you are given three choices below the text for each gap. You should:

- first read the text to get a general understanding of it.
- look carefully at the first gap and ask yourself which word you think could fill it.
- look at the options and choose the best word.
- check that the other options are not correct.
- move on to the next gap.

In Reading **Part 5** you have to fill in the gaps in a text with one word. There are six gaps, but you are not given any choices. The missing words are often 'grammar' words, such as articles (*the, a*), prepositions (for example *in, on, at for*) or words for particular vocabulary. You should:

- first read the text to get a general understanding of it.
- read it again more carefully and fill any gaps you think are easy. But be careful and think of other words that might also fit.
- for the more difficult gaps, note down all the words you think might fit, and choose the best one.

Writing

The Writing part of the test focuses on how well you can communicate in an everyday situation where you need to write a message, and how well you can tell a story. Look at the Model answers for Writing at the back of this book for examples of good written answers.

In Writing **Part 6** you have to write a message which is at least 25 words long. The type of writing could be a note, a text message or an email. This is a test of functional and communicative language. This means you should think about language you use to do things, such as: invite someone to something (*Would you like to ...?*); apologise (*I'm sorry ...*); or ask somebody to do something (*Please would you ... ?*). You should:

- read the question and think carefully about what sort of message you have to write.
- think about functional and communicative language that will help you.
- if you have time, write your message the first time on notepaper and then write it again properly on the answer sheet.
- check that you have included information for each of the points you were asked to.

In Writing **Part 7** you have to look at three pictures and write a story to go with the pictures. The story should be at least 35 words long. It is a good idea to use the simple past tense to tell the story. You need to think about the main things that happen in the story and use joining words (for example, *then, next, after that*) to join them together. You should:

- look at the three pictures and decide what is happening in each picture.
- if you have time, write your story on notepaper the first time and then write the final story on the answer sheet.
- check your use of tenses and joining words.
- make sure you have written about each picture.

Listening

Most of the questions in the listening section are multiple-choice questions. Be careful with multiple-choice questions. Don't just choose the answer option because you see words in an option and you hear the same words. These answers are often not correct. You need to listen to the speakers to see if they accept or reject the options.

In Listening **Part 1** there are five multiple-choice questions. Each question has a written question and three pictures. You have to listen to the audio and choose the correct picture that answers the question. You should:

- read the questions and look at the images first.
- guess the content of each picture. For example, if it is a clock, get ready to hear a time. If there are three different pictures with three different clocks showing three different times, get ready to hear those times.
- listen and choose the best answer the first time the audio is played.
- check your answers the second time the audio is played.

In Listening **Part 2** you have to listen and fill in the gaps in notes. Only one person is speaking. There is only one word (or a time, date or number) to write down. You should:

- read the instructions and the notes.
- think carefully about what the situation is. This will help you fill the gaps. Try to guess words that you think could go in the gap.
- listen to the audio and try to fill the gaps.
- listen again and check your answers.

In Listening **Part 3** you have to listen to two people having an everyday conversation. There are five multiple-choice questions. Each one has three options. You should:

- read the instructions and read through all the questions.
- think carefully about where the conversation is taking place.
- listen to the conversation and choose the best answers.
- listen again and check your answers.

In Listening **Part 4** there are five different questions. For each question you have to listen to a short recording of one or two people talking. There are three options for each question. You have to choose the option that matches the audio. Do not worry if you cannot understand everything you hear. You can still answer the question if you get a general understanding. You should:

- read the instructions carefully and read the questions and options.
- listen and choose the best answers.
- listen again and check your answers.

In Listening **Part 5** there are five questions on one conversation between two speakers. You have to match a person with something and write a letter. To answer this part, you will have to listen to the audio and choose from the answer options. Often the correct answer has the same meaning as the words you hear but uses different words. You should:

- read the instructions carefully and look at the answer options. Think about different words for describing the options, for example if you see the word *guitar* in the answer option, think about the fact that this could be described as a *musical instrument* in the audio.
- think carefully about where the conversation is taking place.
- listen to the audio and choose the best answers.
- listen again and check your answers.

Speaking

You will take your speaking test with another student (sometimes two other students). Try to relax during your speaking test. If you do not understand a question, ask the examiner politely to repeat it. You could say 'Sorry, could you repeat the question please?' You will not lose marks for asking the examiner to repeat their question and it's better than answering the wrong question or not saying anything. Look at the Model answers for Speaking at the back of this book for examples of what good students said in the Speaking test.

In Speaking **Part 1** you have to answer short questions which the examiner asks you. You should:

- answer the questions directly.
- try to give answers of more than one word or sentence.
- don't try to give very long answers in the first part of the test. If you talk for too long the examiner will tell you so don't worry too much about this.

In Speaking **Part 2** you have to talk to the other student and answer more questions from the examiner. In this part it is important to show that you can take part in a conversation. This means you need to show you can listen to another speaker and respond to what they say. You should give your opinion on something and ask for the other student's opinion. You should:

- look carefully at the pictures you have to talk about. Think about what they show and what you like and what you don't like about the things in the picture.
- talk about each picture. Give your opinion, ask the opinion of the other student and say if you agree or disagree with them.
- work to keep the conversation going.
- try to give a longer answer of two or three sentences when the examiner asks you a question. Also give a reason for your answer, for example, 'I like football because ...'.

Dos and don'ts on the test day

- Try not to do last-minute test preparation. Try to relax before your test instead.
- Get to your test centre earlier than you need to, in case there is a problem on the way.

- Don't leave any questions on the test unanswered. You don't lose marks for wrong answers, so make a good guess.
- Don't panic in the test. If you think you have answered one question badly, try to forget about it and make a fresh start with every question.
- Always read the instructions, the questions and the multiple-choice options very carefully.
- In the writing questions, make sure you address all the bullet points or you will lose marks.
- In the speaking part, smile and be communicative and try to keep the conversation going.

Test 1

TEST 1 READING AND WRITING

Part 1

Questions 1–6

For each question, choose the correct answer.

1

SALE!

Buy a swimming costume and get 50% discount on a pair of sunglasses.

A Everything in the shop is half price.

B If you buy a swimming costume, you will pay half price.

C You could pay less if you buy two things.

2

Hi Ellie

I'm going to the photography exhibition on Saturday. Do you want to come? You can buy tickets online. Let me know soon!

Tina

A Ellie needs to buy a ticket soon.

B Ellie needs to tell Tina if she can go to the exhibition.

C Tina needs to buy a ticket online for Ellie.

3

To: Sam
From: Mrs Smith

Sam,

Please meet me in my office to discuss your project. I'm free at 1 p.m. and after the last lesson.

Mrs Smith

A Sam must talk to Mrs Smith about the lesson.

B Mrs Smith is going to teach Sam at 1 p.m.

C Mrs Smith wants to talk to Sam this afternoon.

4

**REPAIRS:
BIKES,
SKATEBOARDS,
SCOOTERS**
Open
Tuesday–Saturday
Closed Sunday–Monday
First repair:
10% discount

A New customers will pay less the first time they go to the shop.

B Customers can buy bikes for less during the week.

C The shop will repair things on Mondays.

5

Hi Tony,

I've uploaded my festival photos. I've shared them on Instagram. The band played really well. Tell me what you think!

Maria

What should Tony do?

A upload his photos from the festival to Instagram

B give Maria his opinion of the photos

C ask Maria to send him the festival photos

6

**WEBSITE-
BUILDING CLUB**

This week's meeting takes place at 3.30 p.m. in the library, not the computer room.

A The place where the club meets is different this week.

B The club meets in different rooms and at different times every week.

C The club will not meet in the computer room anymore.

Part 2

Questions 7–13

For each question, choose the correct answer.

		Jenny	Megan	Maria
7	Who went on holiday with her friends?	A	B	C
8	Who says that it can be boring to go on long journeys?	A	B	C
9	Who made a mistake with her shoes?	A	B	C
10	Who did something she enjoys while she was waiting?	A	B	C
11	Who had fun even though the weather was bad?	A	B	C
12	Who missed an enjoyable experience with her friends?	A	B	C
13	Who says they often travel?	A	B	C

Travel experiences

Jenny

My family and I go on holiday to faraway places a lot. I spend hours in airports and on planes, and sometimes I get bored. Last winter we went to Singapore. When we arrived at the airport in Manchester, there was a terrible thunderstorm and our flight was delayed for five hours. Luckily, I had my laptop and my camera with me. I like making videos of our trips, so I kept busy and the time went quickly.

Megan

Last June, I went to the UK to study at a language school. There were people there from all over the world and I made some new friends. One Saturday, we went to a music festival. It was in a field in the countryside. It was a sunny day, so I wore my new sandals. That was a mistake. It started raining at midday and it never stopped. My feet got wet, cold and muddy. However, I enjoyed myself, and the music was brilliant. Next time I'll wear boots!

Maria

Last summer I went on a school trip to London. On the first day we went sightseeing, but there were a lot of people everywhere because the city is so popular, so we had to queue a lot. We walked all day and my feet were tired by the end of the day. That evening I decided to stay in the hotel to rest. While I was in the hotel, my friends went on an exciting night tour of the city – on a bus!

Part 3

Questions 14–18

For each question, choose the correct answer.

The first musical instrument

by Jared Keene, age 12

Music has been an important part of people's lives for thousands of years. Long before musicians wrote music, people were playing their own instruments and making music.
Some of the oldest instruments ever found are more than 40,000 years old! They're flutes, and they come from a cave in the south of Germany. Instruments like flutes are called wind instruments; you play them by blowing air into them with your mouth. The flutes in the cave were long and thin with small holes.

There were also many paintings on the walls of the cave. They are some of the oldest paintings in the world and they show people in their daily lives. The paintings help us learn about life in the past. Scientists believe that thousands of years ago, people sat around fires and played the flutes for entertainment. They shared songs and music together. This helped them to build friendships.

When scientists found the first flute, they didn't know what it was because it was broken. One scientist, Maria Malina, thought it might be an instrument, so she put the pieces together. And she was right! The flute was made from the bone of a bird's leg. When people played the flutes, they found that they could play five different notes – five different sounds – just like music today. It's impossible to know what kind of music people played thousands of years ago, but now we know what one instrument sounded like!

14 What is the text about?

    A very old cave paintings

    B how to make a musical instrument

    C a kind of musical instrument

15 The flutes in the cave are special because

    A there aren't many in the world.

    B they come from Germany.

    C they are very old.

16 The paintings in the cave show

    A how people lived in the past.

    B how the flutes were made.

    C the kind of songs people sang.

17 At first, scientists didn't know the instrument was a flute because

    A it was in pieces.

    B the pieces were from a bird's leg.

    C no one had seen an ancient flute before.

18 Today we know

    A the kind of music that people played thousands of years ago.

    B the sound that flutes made thousands of years ago.

    C that people played only five notes thousands of years ago.

Part 4

Questions 19–24

For each question, choose the correct answer.

Greta Thunberg

Greta Thunberg was born in Sweden. At 16 years old, she started a group of **(19)** .... people against climate change. Greta was **(20)** .... about the terrible things happening to our planet. She thought people weren't doing enough to solve them. So, in August 2018, Greta and a group of students had a **(21)** .... in the centre of Stockholm. Greta wanted journalists and people around the world to listen to the group. It was a difficult **(22)** ....! But with the help of social media, people started listening. Then, in December 2018, Greta got her chance to speak at the UN climate meeting in Poland. Many people around the world have become **(23)** .... in her work. Greta knows it isn't going to be easy to change the world. But she **(24)** .... that we can all make a difference.

19	**A** little	**B** small	**C** young
20	**A** worried	**B** afraid	**C** bored
21	**A** lesson	**B** meeting	**C** appointment
22	**A** job	**B** career	**C** work
23	**A** important	**B** careful	**C** interested
24	**A** tells	**B** believes	**C** guesses

Part 5

Questions 25–30

For each question, write the correct answer.
Write **one** word for each gap.

Example: | **0** | *for* |

EMAIL	
From:	Prisha
To:	Cara

Hi Cara,

Thanks **(0)** .... your email and the photos of your hometown. I enjoy reading **(25)** .... your life in Edinburgh. It's very different from my life in New Delhi. I was interested to learn that you have the same hobby **(26)** .... me. I love collecting old photos, **(27)** .... Can **(28)** .... send me one from Scotland? I have photos of Delhi, Tokyo, Hong Kong, New York **(29)** .... London. My favourite is one of the Red Fort in New Delhi. It's from 1858! What **(30)** .... your favourite photos?

Please write soon!
Prisha

Part 6

Question 31

You want to go to the cinema on Saturday with your English friend Ben. Write an email to Ben.

In your email:
- ask Ben to go to the cinema on Saturday
- say which cinema you want to go to
- say how you will travel there.

Write **25 words** or more.

Write the email on your answer sheet.

Part 7

Question 32

Look at the three pictures.
Write the story shown in the pictures.
Write **35 words** or more.

Write the story on your answer sheet.

TEST 1 LISTENING

Part 1

Questions 1–5

For each question, choose the correct answer.

---

1 Which is the most popular place?

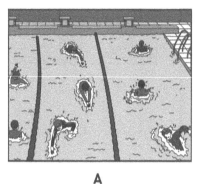

A

B

C

2 What does John like to do on the bus to school?

A

B

C

3 When does the girl have a geography lesson?

Tuesday	Thursday	Friday
A	B	C

4 When does badminton practice usually start?

A   B   C

5 What present will they buy?

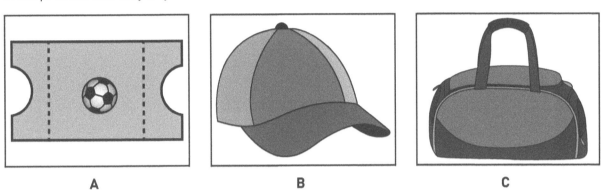

A   B   C

Part 2

02

Questions 6–10

For each question, write the correct answer in the gap. Write **one word** or **a number** or **a date** or **a time**.

You will hear a woman talking to some people about a new library.

Library Information for Students	
Opening date:	Saturday 5th June
Usual opening hours:	8 a.m. to **(6)** ....
Friday summer closing time:	**(7)** ....
Travel time	By bus **(8)** .... minutes from city centre
Bus ticket price:	**(9)** ....
Office phone number:	**(10)** ....

Part 3

Questions 11–15

For each question, choose the correct answer.

You will hear Tom talking to his dad about his birthday party.

11 How does Tom's dad feel about the party at first?

A He thinks it's a great idea.

B He's unsure about the idea.

C He doesn't think there is any need for it.

12 How many friends does Tom want to invite?

A thirteen

B fourteen

C twenty-five

13 Eva's mother is from

A the UK.

B the USA.

C Brazil.

14 Where was Eva's party?

A at a disco

B at a restaurant

C at home

15 Tom's dad says that they

A don't have to invite all the family.

B have to invite the neighbours.

C have to invite everyone they know.

Part 4

Questions 16–20

For each question, choose the correct answer.

---

16   You will hear a customer talking to a shop assistant.
     Why does he want to return the jacket?

   A   There is something wrong with it.

   B   It isn't big enough for him.

   C   It is the wrong colour.

17   You will hear a girl talking about her best friend, Danielle.
     What does Danielle look like?

   A   She has long hair and blue eyes.

   B   She has short hair and green eyes.

   C   She has dark hair and green eyes.

18   You will hear a girl talking to her dentist.
     Why is she unhappy?

   A   She has broken her tooth.

   B   She has a toothache.

   C   She has lost a lot of blood.

19   You will hear two friends talking about their plans.
     What do they decide to do at the weekend?

   A   go shopping

   B   watch TV

   C   go to the beach

20   You will hear a mother talking to her son, Harry.
     What does Harry's mum ask him to do?

   A   tidy his bedroom

   B   throw the rubbish out

   C   fix his skateboard

Part 5

05

Questions 21–25

For each question, choose the correct answer.

You will hear Billy talking to Lucy about a camping trip.
What will each person bring to the camp?

Example:

0 Lucy ☐ **D**

People		Items
21 Mark ☐		**A** knives and forks
22 Billy ☐		**B** lamp
23 Alicia ☐		**C** tent
24 Tina ☐		**D** food
25 Emma ☐		**E** torch
		F sleeping bags
		G cups
		H gas cooker

You now have six minutes to write your answers on the answer sheet.

TEST 1 SPEAKING

You are Candidate B. Answer the questions.

06–07

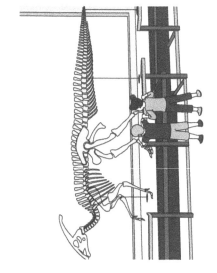

Do you like these different free-time activities?

Audio scripts and Model answers on pages 167–223.

Test 2

TEST 2 READING AND WRITING

Part 1

01

Questions 1–6

For each question, choose the correct answer.

1

John,

Dad's taken the car to the garage. There's money for you on the table so you can catch the bus to school.

Love, Mum

A Dad will drive John to school.

B John will need money to get to school.

C Mum wants John to give the money to Dad.

2

STUDENTS
SCHOOL TRIP
Your parents must complete the forms. Please return them by Friday.

A Students can only return the forms on Friday.

B Students' parents must return the forms.

C Students can't go on the trip if their parents don't complete the forms.

3

To: Jason
From: Emma

Jason,

I have tickets to the music festival.

It starts at 10 a.m. but let's meet at the train station earlier.

Emma

A Jason will meet Emma before ten o'clock.

B Emma will meet Jason at the station at ten o'clock.

C Jason will buy tickets for the festival before ten o'clock.

4

Badminton coach

£15 an hour
Beginners can borrow
equipment.
Please wear trainers.

A Some people don't pay for lessons.

B Everyone must wear the right type of shoes.

C Beginners must bring a racket to lessons.

5

Kyle,

I need a Saturday job. How do I start?

Please tell me what to do.

Sam

What should Kyle do?

A Give Sam a job.

B Tell Sam about his job.

C Give Sam some advice.

6

Classroom rules

Please wear a white
coat and safety glasses
before entering the
science lab.

A Put on the right clothes and then go into the lab.

B Enter the lab and then put on the right clothes.

C Wear your school uniform during science lessons.

Part 2

Questions 7–13

For each question, choose the correct answer.

		Ahmed	Victor	Christophe
7	Who prefers being outside in his free time?	A	B	C
8	Who learned a skill from a parent?	A	B	C
9	Who does a sport as a hobby?	A	B	C
10	Who has a hobby that is different from his friends' hobbies?	A	B	C
11	Who has a hobby that helps others?	A	B	C
12	Who won something doing their hobby?	A	B	C
13	Who says that people have told him they like what he does?	A	B	C

Three teenagers talk about their hobbies

Ahmed

I spend very little of my free time indoors. I take part in marathons and I make videos about running. I have a YouTube channel where I upload them, and I have many followers. I love running and the videos give me a chance to share my training with others. It's great to read the comments that people leave. They say they are better runners after they watch the videos.

Victor

I don't remember when I learned to cook. Mum says I started when I was five years old. I watched her as she prepared our meals and I quickly became good at it because I practised my cooking skills every day. At the weekend, I use my free time to learn new recipes. I enjoy cooking for my family, and I put pictures of my meals online. The good thing about being the chef is you don't have to wash up afterwards. My sister does that!

Christophe

My friends enjoy writing blogs in their spare time and my brother loves doing sports outside, but I prefer to make things. I'm a member of the science club at school. Last month, we entered a competition. The school with the best ideas was invited to a science fair in London. And that was my school! We made a 3D-printer. You can make anything you like with it. The judges really liked our printer and we got first prize! We were so happy! Our parents were at the fair and they were very proud of us.

Part 3

Questions 14–18

For each question, choose the correct answer.

A school for all

by Karen Green, 13

Most children have lessons in a school building, but there are some parts of the world where students don't learn in buildings. Their schools are in very unusual places. The Hope Bus in Iraq is one such school.

After years of war, many Iraqi children couldn't go to school. They didn't have books, pens or pencils. A lot of school buildings were damaged or unsafe. Unfortunately, it is expensive to build new schools and it also takes a long time to build them. It is also dangerous and difficult for Iraqi children to travel to school.

Then, one day, a group of people had an idea. They decided to make a school where all children could learn. If the children couldn't travel to school, the school would travel to them. So they bought an old bus and gave it a makeover. First, they painted the outside in a bright colour. Then they changed the inside. They took out the bus seats and added 20 desks – enough for 50 students. They also added a TV and a blackboard for the teachers. The bus became a school on wheels.

Today, the Hope Bus travels around Iraq's capital city, Baghdad. Children can sit inside and learn in a quiet and safe place. They can learn both English and Arabic and they can make lots of new friends. The team who created the Hope Bus want to make twelve more buses to give all children an education and a better future.

14 What does the writer say in the first paragraph?

    A   The Hope Bus is in an unusual part of the world.

    B   The Hope Bus is different from other schools.

    C   The Hope Bus is a very strange building.

15 Many Iraqi children

    A   didn't have anywhere to learn.

    B   had safe places to live.

    C   wanted more modern schools.

16 What is special about the Hope Bus?

    A   Children can easily travel to it.

    B   Teachers can get to school quickly.

    C   The school can travel to the children.

17 The people who made the Hope Bus changed it by

    A   putting in equipment and giving students somewhere to sit.

    B   adding many more seats inside the bus.

    C   giving each student a TV and a blackboard.

18 What do the people who made the Hope Bus want?

    A   They want more children to use the Hope Bus.

    B   They want to help more children learn.

    C   They want schools in Baghdad to make their own buses.

Part 4

Questions 19–24

For each question, choose the correct answer.

Marie Skłodowska Curie

Marie Skłodowska was born in Poland in 1867. She was very **(19)** .... but because she was a girl she couldn't go to university in Poland. In 1891, she **(20)** .... to Paris to study physics and mathematics.

In 1894, Marie **(21)** .... another scientist, Pierre Curie. They got married and they did a lot of important scientific work together. In 1897, Marie and Pierre's daughter, Irène, was **(22)** ....

In 1903, Marie and Pierre won the Nobel Prize in Physics. This is one of the most **(23)** .... prizes in the world for science and Marie was the first woman to win one.

In 1904, Pierre had a terrible **(24)** .... and died, but Marie carried on working in science, and in 1911 she won a second Nobel prize, this time in chemistry.

19	**A** rich	**B** famous	**C** clever
20	**A** moved	**B** lived	**C** left
21	**A** met	**B** knew	**C** learnt
22	**A** grown	**B** born	**C** made
23	**A** terrible	**B** modern	**C** important
24	**A** appointment	**B** ambulance	**C** accident

Part 5

Questions 25–30

For each question, write the correct answer.
Write **one** word for each gap.

Example: | **0** | *for* |

EMAIL

From: Leon

To: Phil

Hi Phil,

My family and I went to Germany **(0)** .... three days in April. We don't really like beach holidays, so we took a trip to Berlin instead. When we go **(25)** .... holiday, we usually visit lots of museums but we didn't have time **(26)** .... see everything this time. We went to the Berlin Wall and the Brandenburg Gate. We read **(27)** .... them in a guidebook before we visited them. They **(28)** .... both really interesting.

What kind of holidays **(29)** .... you like – beach holidays **(30)** .... city trips?

Write back soon.

Leon

Part 6

Question 31

You are going camping with your English friend Alex this weekend.
Write an email to Alex.

In your email:

- say what time is a good time to meet
- tell him what to bring
- say what activities you can do while camping.

Write **25 words** or more.

Write the email on your answer sheet.

Part 7

Question 32

Look at the three pictures.
Write the story shown in the pictures.
Write **35 words** or more.

Write the story on your answer sheet.

TEST 2 LISTENING

Part 1

Questions 1–5

For each question, choose the correct answer.

---

1   Who is the girl's brother?

A

B

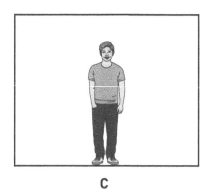

C

2   What project did Kim finish for school?

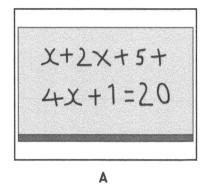

A

B

C

3   What will Mark have for lunch?

A

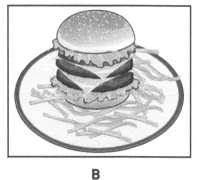

B

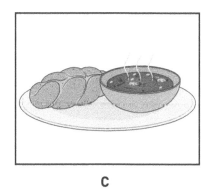

C

4 What time does Sam's hockey lesson start?

A

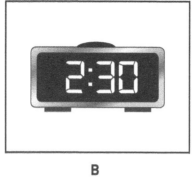

B

C

5 Which building is nearest to them?

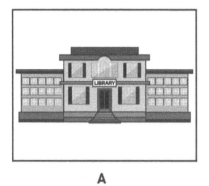

A

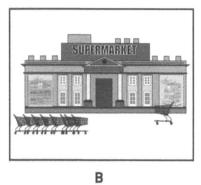

B

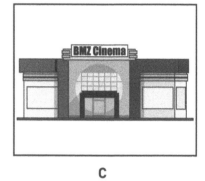

C

Part 2

09

Questions 6–10

For each question, write the correct answer in the gap. Write **one word** or **a number** or **a date** or **a time**.

You will hear a boy telling people about his business.

Henry Divani

Age:	14
Started at the age of:	**(6)** ....
Title of book:	The Adventures of **(7)** ....
Price:	£9.99 and then **(8)** £ ....
Sold:	10,000 copies in the first month and **(9)** .... in the second month
Starts writing:	at **(10)** .... every morning

10

Part 3

Questions 11–15

For each question, choose the correct answer.

You will hear Lily talking on the phone to her friend Ethan about an accident.

11 What happened to Ethan in the accident?

    A He broke his foot.

    B He cut his head.

    C He hurt his arm.

12 How did Ethan go to hospital?

    A An ambulance took him there.

    B He went there by car.

    C His neighbour drove him there.

13 Ethan can't go to school for

    A a month.

    B a week.

    C a few days.

14 What will Ethan probably do at home?

    A He will play video games.

    B He will watch TV all day.

    C He will study and do homework.

15 Lily offers to

    A come and see Ethan.

    B do Ethan's homework for him.

    C help Ethan with lessons at school.

Part 4

11

Questions 16–20

For each question, choose the correct answer.

---

16 You will hear two friends talking about the best way to go home.
Which is the shortest way?

    A across the fields

    B over the hill

    C around the lake

17 You will hear Ivan talking to his friend Megan.
What did Megan do about her problem?

    A She went swimming.

    B She did some special exercises.

    C She changed her trainers.

18 You will hear a girl talking to a shop assistant.
What can't she do?

    A leave one skirt with the shop assistant

    B try on more than five skirts

    C go into the changing room at this time

19 You will hear a boy talking to his mother.
What does she want him to do?

    A start washing his football kit

    B stop buying expensive football boots

    C take care of his football boots

20 You will hear a teacher talking to a student.
Why is he talking to her?

    A to ask her if he can share her work

    B to ask her to make a school website

    C to ask her to do a project about their town

Part 5

12

Questions 21–25

For each question, choose the correct answer.

You will hear Tom and Ivy planning what they would like to do in the school holidays.
What activity will they do on each day?

Example:

0   Monday | E |

Days		**Activities**
21 Tuesday ☐		**A** zoo
22 Wednesday ☐		**B** castle
23 Thursday ☐		**C** beach
24 Friday ☐		**D** market
25 Saturday ☐		**E** boat trip
		F guided tour
		G museum
		H shopping

You now have six minutes to write your answers on the answer sheet.

Test 2 SPEAKING

You are Candidate B. Answer the questions.

13–14

Do you like these different types of holiday?

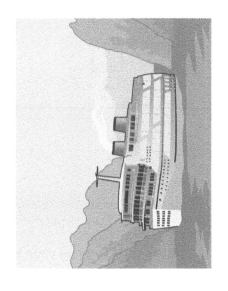

Audio scripts and Model answers on pages 167–223.

Test 3

TEST 3 READING AND WRITING

Part 1

Questions 1–6

For each question, choose the correct answer.

1

SAILING TRIP

To go on the trip, you must be able to swim well.

A The trip is only for good swimmers.

B People on the trip must be good at sailing.

C Swimmers of all levels can go on the trip.

2

Harry,

I've got some ideas for our science project. Can we discuss them tonight? Do you have any free time for a video chat?

Zara

What does Harry need to do?

A Give Zara ideas for the project.

B Call Zara tonight.

C Tell Zara if he can talk tonight.

3

The school will stay closed next week on Monday 12th for teacher training.

A The school is closed for a week.

B Only teachers can go to the school on Monday.

C No one can go to the school on Monday.

4

> **Bird Theatre**
> Drama club for 12- to
> 14-year-olds starts on
> 10th July

A   The drama club is only for people aged 12 and 14.

B   Children can watch a play about birds on 10th July.

C   The first meeting of the drama club will take place on 10th July.

5

> **To:** Anna
> **From:** Kim
>
> Anna,
>
> I made a mistake! My party starts at 8, not 7. Can you bring some drinks and pizza?
>
> Kim

A   Anna thinks it is a mistake to have a party.

B   Kim needs some things for the party.

C   The party will be on a different day and at a different time.

6

> **FAIR**
> **Bring books and toys you don't want and sell them at our stall.**

A   The stall will have new books and toys for sale.

B   You can sell anything at the fair.

C   People will be able to buy old things from the stall.

Part 2

Questions 7–13

For each question, choose the correct answer.

		Adam	Kaito	José
7	Who uses public transport to go to school?	A	B	C
8	Who describes one of the meals he has every day?	A	B	C
9	Who plays two sports?	A	B	C
10	Who helps a parent with their work after school?	A	B	C
11	Who makes a meal for his family?	A	B	C
12	Who does school work in the evening?	A	B	C
13	Who has the shortest school day?	A	B	C

Three teens and their everyday lives

Adam

I live on a farm in New Zealand. I wake up at six and have a big breakfast: bacon, eggs, orange juice and toast. My mother takes care of the animals on the farm. My father is a teacher and we ride our bikes to school together instead of taking the bus. School starts at eight and finishes at three. Dad and I help Mum on the farm before we have an early dinner. In the evenings, I play video games and then I go to bed.

Kaito

I live in a village on the Japanese island of Honshu. I get up at seven and walk to school with my friends. Lessons begin at half past eight and finish at three. After that, I go to an after-school club. I play badminton and table tennis, but you can also do things like folk dancing and baseball. When my parents come home from work, Dad makes dinner and we eat together. Then I study for a few hours before I go to bed.

José

I live in Mexico City. I get up at six and catch a bus to school half an hour later. Lessons start at half past seven. We have a break at ten and then we carry on until half past twelve. I get home at quarter to two. After that, I go to the sports centre with my friends to play football. In the evenings I cook dinner for my family. Then I listen to music before bed at nine thirty.

Part 3

Questions 14–18

For each question, choose the correct answer.

Summer job: Ideas and help

by Jake Summers

The school summer holidays are the perfect time of year to get a part-time job. You will have the chance to earn money and get some useful experience. Many businesses like to give jobs to young people because they learn new skills quickly. Not sure which job would be best for you? Here are some ideas to get you started.

Do you like helping people?
What about working with the elderly? It's a really good way of giving something back to your community. You can help old people do simple jobs. For example, they might need someone to help them at the supermarket, use a computer, do the washing up or do the gardening. You can also just sit with them, playing games and keeping them company.

Can you play cricket, hockey or another sport?
Do you like teaching people new skills? Then a job as an assistant sports coach would be a brilliant summer job. You could spend all summer in your football boots or hitting a ball on a tennis court! Coaching will also give you experience of working with young children, which is great if you want to be a teacher one day.

Are you interested in technology?
There are many technology companies that have training programmes for young people where you can learn lots of useful IT skills. You could even see how game designers and engineers create video games. This is great if you want to study IT or other computer-related courses in the future at university.

14 When is it a good idea to get a part-time job?

    A after school

    B all year

    C during the summer

15 You can help elderly people

    A at work.

    B at home.

    C at the sports centre.

16 To be an assistant sports coach,

    A you have to be brilliant at sport.

    B you must learn some new skills.

    C you must be able to play a sport.

17 What job could you do in the future if you like coaching?

    A a teacher

    B a sportsperson

    C a sports shop assistant

18 What can you learn at a technology company?

    A how to teach others

    B how to make computers

    C IT skills

Part 4

Questions 19–24

For each question, choose the correct answer.

Hadrian's Wall

Hadrian's Wall is an ancient stone wall in the north of England. It is about 120 **(19)** .... long and goes from the Irish Sea in the west, across the country to the North Sea in the east. It was built by the ancient Romans over 2,000 years ago to stop people from the north **(20)** .... the country. It **(21)** .... over fourteen years to build and was the largest structure the Romans ever made. Today, you can see only small parts of the wall. After the Romans left Britain, people used the stones to build castles, churches and other buildings. Then in the 19th **(22)** ...., archaeologists and historians become **(23)** .... in the parts of the wall that were left and tried to **(24)** .... after it.

19	**A** litres	**B** kilometres	**C** kilogrammes
20	**A** travelling	**B** coming	**C** entering
21	**A** took	**B** used	**C** got
22	**A** age	**B** century	**C** year
23	**A** bored	**B** worried	**C** interested
24	**A** look	**B** watch	**C** find

Part 5

Questions 25–30

For each question, write the correct answer.
Write **one** word for each gap.

61

Example: | **0** | *for* |

EMAIL
From: Alice
To: George

Thank you **(0)** .... your email. It's really interesting to find out about life in other places. In Singapore, it's often hot all year round and we have many thunderstorms. It's usually warm **(25)** .... wet and it doesn't get cold very often. The weather **(26)** .... windy in spring, from March **(27)** .... May. It also rains a lot! There are about 170 rainy days a year.

What's the weather like where **(28)** .... live? **(29)** .... it snow a lot in winter? When do you have hot weather during **(30)** .... year?

Write back soon,
Alice

Part 6

Question 31

You want to join your English friend Jacob's chess club.
Write an email to Jacob.

In your email:

- ask Jacob when the members of the chess club meet
- ask how often the members play chess at the club
- say if you have played chess before.

Write **25 words** or more.

Write the email on your answer sheet.

Part 7

Question 32

Look at the three pictures.
Write the story shown in the pictures.
Write **35 words** or more.

Write the story on your answer sheet.

TEST 3 LISTENING

Part 1

15

Questions 1–5

For each question, choose the correct answer.

---

1   Where do they think the boy left his phone?

A

B

C

2   How did the family celebrate Lisa's grandmother's birthday?

A

B

C

3   Who got the cat off the roof?

A

B

C

4 Which photo won the competition?

A   B   C

5 What time does the film start?

A   B   C

Part 2

16

Questions 6–10

For each question, write the correct answer in the gap. Write **one word** or **a number** or **a date** or **a time**.

You will hear a teacher talking to a group of students about a camping trip.

School camping trip

Day:	Saturday
Departure time:	**(6)** .... in the morning
Meet:	at the **(7)** .... building
Days:	Saturday morning until **(8)** .... evening
Journey time:	**(9)** .... hours
Items to bring:	A **(10)** ...., a bottle of water, comfortable shoes, sun cream

17

Part 3

Questions 11–15

For each question, choose the correct answer.

You will hear Oscar talking to his friend Emily about going to a concert.

11 What kind of music will they hear at the concert?

    A pop and classical

    B rock and pop

    C rock and classical

12 Oscar and Emily will go to the concert hall by

    A car.

    B bus.

    C train.

13 Tom

    A doesn't live far from the concert hall.

    B is going to the concert hall by bus.

    C will take the train or walk.

14 Oscar says that

    A Tom will buy the tickets for them.

    B there are hundreds of tickets available.

    C they must arrive at the concert hall early.

15 Where does Oscar suggest going after the concert?

    A somewhere to eat

    B to Tom's house

    C shopping in town

Questions 11–15

Part 4

18

Questions 16–20

For each question, choose the correct answer.

---

16 You will hear a man talking about feeling ill.
What did he do?

    A   He got lots of rest.

    B   He went to the doctor.

    C   He took some medicine.

17 You will hear a boy talking to his friend Sue.
What did Sue forget to buy?

    A   meat for the barbecue

    B   snacks and desserts

    C   vegetables

18 You will hear two friends talking about a club.
Why is Joseph talking to Katie?

    A   He wants information about the club.

    B   He's telling Katie why she should join the club.

    C   He's asking for ideas about summer clubs.

19 You will hear two friends talking.
Where are they?

    A   at school

    B   at a department store

    C   at a post office

20 You will hear two friends talking.
Where will they go first?

    A   to the underground

    B   to the airport

    C   to the bus stop

Part 5

19

Questions 21–25

For each question, choose the correct answer.

You will hear Matt talking to a friend about different hobbies.
Which hobby does each person do?

Example:

Dylan | G |

People		Hobbies
21 Sam	☐	**A** gardening
22 Eva	☐	**B** playing an instrument
23 Kim	☐	**C** acting
24 Max	☐	**D** camping
25 Ellie	☐	**E** fishing
		F listening to music
		G photography
		H sailing

You now have six minutes to write your answers on the answer sheet.

Test 3 SPEAKING

You are Candidate B. Answer the questions.

20–21

Do you like these types of exercise?

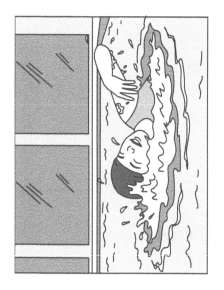

Audio scripts and Model answers on pages 167–223.

Test 4

TEST 4 READING AND WRITING

Part 1

Questions 1–6

For each question, choose the correct answer.

1

> **To:** All new students
>
> **From**: School Office
>
> Please complete the form from your teacher with information about yourself and return it to us by Friday.

A You have to return the form to the school office by the end of the week.

B Your teacher will complete a form with information about you.

C You need to return the form to your teacher by Friday.

2

> Julia,
>
> What do you need for your cooking lesson? How much sugar and butter? I'm shopping now so tell me what you need.
>
> Mum

What should Julia do?

A buy things for her cooking lesson

B tell her mum what she needs for her lesson

C go shopping with her mum for ingredients

3

> Free furniture – desk, computer chair, lamp, shelves. Please take anything you need.
>
> Thank you!

A You must pay for anything you need.

B You don't need to pay for the furniture.

C You can leave any of your own furniture that you don't need.

4

No talking outside
this room while
examinations are
taking place
9–11 this morning.

A You mustn't talk while you are taking an exam.

B You can't talk in the room between 9 and 11.

C You need to be quiet while you are passing the room.

5

Danger!
Please be careful when
leaving the building.
There is ice on the
ground.

A The area outside the building is dangerous.

B The building has ice on the floor.

C The floors in the building are wet.

6

Tom,

Ian isn't well so
he's isn't going
to band practice.

I'll go if you go,
so let me know
your plans.

Samir

A Samir isn't well so he doesn't want to go to band practice.

B Samir wants to go to band practice with Tom.

C Samir and Ian won't go to band practice today.

Part 2

Questions 7–13

For each question, choose the correct answer.

		Ruby	Beth	Sienna
7	Who doesn't buy clothes from the Internet?	A	B	C
8	Who doesn't spend a lot of money on clothes?	A	B	C
9	Who thinks about the people who make the clothes she buys?	A	B	C
10	Who prefers buying clothes at markets?	A	B	C
11	Who wants to have a job in fashion one day?	A	B	C
12	Who enjoys showing other people her clothes?	A	B	C
13	Who thinks people should wear their clothes many times?	A	B	C

Young people and fashion

Ruby

Ruby doesn't buy lots of clothes from shops in her town centre because she thinks they look too similar. She goes to street markets or second-hand clothes shops to buy clothes. For her, fashion means unusual, older clothes that you can't find on the high street. She doesn't like wearing clothes only a few times and then throwing them away. Instead, she likes to buy clothes that you can wear for a long time. She also thinks it is important to know where your clothes are made.

Beth

Beth likes to wear sports clothes, but they are often expensive in shopping centres. She hasn't got enough money to buy them, so she waits for the sales. She usually buys clothes online because there is a larger variety to choose from and the prices are lower. Beth also likes making videos about her clothes and posting them on social media. She has many followers on YouTube. She wants other young people to learn how they can look good and spend less money.

Sienna

Fashion is important to Sienna. But it is also important to her that clothes are good for the environment and that the workers in the factories earn enough money. She doesn't buy cheap clothes from big shops or shopping centres. She prefers to buy them from small shops on the Internet or in her town. Sienna also enjoys making her own clothes. She wants to be a fashion designer in the future.

Part 3

Questions 14–18

For each question, choose the correct answer.

A full-time job in e-sports

by Neville Forrester

There are more young people playing video games around the world than ever before. It is a fun hobby and now, for some, it is also a big business. In 2019 over 12,000 fans were in a stadium in London, watching a game. But this wasn't an ordinary sports game. This was an e-sports game and the prize money for the winners was over £3 million.

Over the last few years, many people have chosen to change their hobby into a job. They have become full-time gamers and play in big competitions, winning lots of prize money too. They usually practise for ten or more hours a day, five or six days a week.

As well as playing games, many people like watching them. Video websites like Twitch and YouTube have become popular places to watch games, and in the UK there is a TV channel showing e-sports 24 hours a day. They can be exciting to watch – just like other sports.

However, many people ask: are e-sports really sports? Are the players athletes? Some say no because e-sports players don't need to run, jump, throw or move. But others say yes because players need lots of skills to win.

In China and South Korea, the government classify e-sports as sports, and people will play them in the Asian Games from 2022. They are certainly very popular and it looks like they will be important in the future.

14 What did many people watch in London in 2019?

    A a sports match

    B a video game

    C an e-sports game

15 People who play video games as a job

    A have become well known.

    B practise for many hours.

    C don't make a lot of money.

16 Where do people watch e-sports games?

    A always on the Internet

    B in different ways

    C only on TV

17 Some people think that

    A e-sports keep you active.

    B anyone can be an e-sports player.

    C e-sports isn't a sport.

18 At the Asian Games in 2022,

    A people will be able to watch e-sports.

    B e-sports games will be the most popular events.

    C China and Korea will make e-sports real sports.

Part 4

Questions 19–24

For each question, choose the correct answer.

Braille

All over the world, blind people, who don't have the ability to see, use a **(19)** .... of writing called Braille. Braille doesn't use letters; it uses raised dots. There are 63 combinations of dots, and each group of dots stands for a different letter, number, punctuation mark or word. It lets people **(20)** .... by touch – by using their **(21)** .... to feel.

Braille is a code, so people can use it to write in different **(22)** .... It is called Braille because a Frenchman, Louis Braille, invented it. Louis lost his sight when he was **(23)** ...., after an accident. Because he was blind, he went to school at the Royal Institute for Blind Children in France. He was very intelligent and he invented the code at the **(24)** .... of 15.

19	**A** plan	**B** way	**C** path
20	**A** read	**B** speak	**C** talk
21	**A** toes	**B** arms	**C** fingers
22	**A** lessons	**B** languages	**C** subjects
23	**A** new	**B** early	**C** young
24	**A** time	**B** age	**C** number

Part 5

Questions 25–30

For each question, write the correct answer.
Write **one** word for each gap.

Example: | **0** | *a* |

> **EMAIL**
>
> From: | Joe
>
> To: | Luca
>
> I don't have **(0)** .... big family. I live with
> **(25)** .... parents in an apartment. I don't have
> **(26)** .... brothers or sisters, but I have two
> cousins, Emma and Andy. They're my neighbours, too!
> They live in **(27)** .... same building as me. Emma
> is nine and Andy is twelve years old. Emma loves
> animals and listening **(28)** .... music. Andy is
> a big fan **(29)** .... football. We spend a
> **(30)** .... of time together at their house. Their
> mum, my aunt, is a musician. Their house is full of
> musical instruments and books. It's amazing!
>
> Write and tell me about your family,
>
> Joe

Part 6

Question 31

You are going to a party on Saturday with your English friend, Alex.
Write an email to Alex.

In your email:

- ask Alex what time he wants to meet

- say what clothes you are going to wear

- say if you are going to bring any food or drink to the party.

Write **25 words** or more.

Write the email on your answer sheet.

Part 7

Question 32

Look at the three pictures.
Write the story shown in the pictures.
Write **35 words** or more.

Write the story on your answer sheet.

TEST 4 LISTENING

Part 1

Questions 1–5

For each question, choose the correct answer.

---

1 What is Tom's new Saturday job?

A

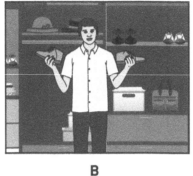

B

C

2 What does the girl want for lunch?

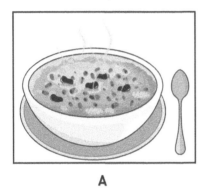

A

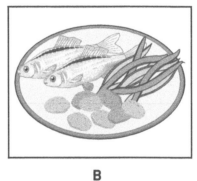

B

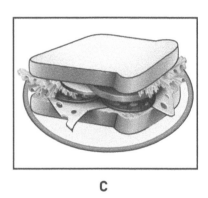

C

3 Where is the boy's tent?

A

B

C

4 How does Sue usually communicate with Pablo?

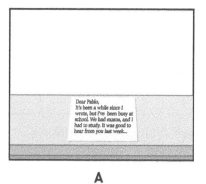

Dear Pablo,
It's been a while since I wrote, but I've been busy at school. We had exams, and I had to study. It was good to hear from you last week...

A

Hi Pablo,
I saw this magazine and I thought of you. It's got some good articles.

B

C

5 What did Alex forget to bring to school?

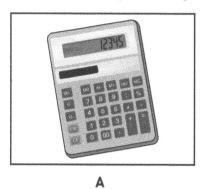

A

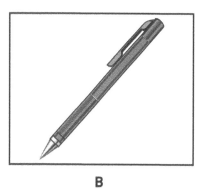

B

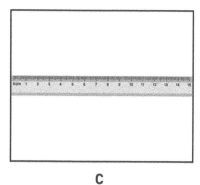

C

Part 2

Questions 6–10

For each question, write the correct answer in the gap. Write **one word** or **a number** or **a date** or **a time**.

You will hear a teacher talking to a group of students about a student exchange programme.

Student exchange programme

Number of weeks:	Two
Place:	**(6)** .... in France
Dates:	In France: **(7)** .... to 10th March. In the UK: 11th to 17th March
Ages:	**(8)** .... to 13 years old
Spending money:	**(9)** £...........
All meals:	with **(10)** ....

Part 3

Questions 11–15

For each question, choose the correct answer.

You will hear a girl talking on the phone to a staff member at a train station about a train ticket.

11 Where is the girl going?

    A   Liverpool

    B   London

    C   Crewe

12 When does the next train arrive in Crewe?

    A   11.13

    B   12.01

    C   15.31

13 Where can't people buy a ticket today?

    A   from the train station

    B   from a ticket machine

    C   on the Internet

14 How much will the girl pay?

    A   £21.10

    B   £32.00

    C   £41.00

15 The girl will pay for her ticket

    A   over the phone.

    B   on the train.

    C   at the station.

Part 4

25

Questions 16–20

For each question, choose the correct answer.

---

16 You will hear a brother and sister talking.
Where did the girl leave her glasses?

   A in her bedroom

   B in the kitchen

   C in the living room

17 You will hear two friends talking about reading.
How does the girl prefer to read?

   A books

   B articles on her laptop

   C e-books

18 You will hear two friends talking in a café.
What does the boy want to eat?

   A pasta salad

   B a burger and chips

   C a chicken sandwich

19 You will hear a girl talking on the phone.
Why is she happy?

   A She is going on holiday.

   B Her cousin is coming to visit her.

   C She is going to visit her aunt and uncle.

20 You will hear a boy talking to his friend about his summer job.
Where was his job?

   A a café

   B a farm

   C a fruit and vegetable market

Part 5

26

Questions 21–25

For each question, choose the correct answer.

You will hear Tom talking to his friend Sarah about an international festival at their school. What will each person do for the festival?

Example:

Max | B |

People		**Activity**

People

21   Megan

22   Ruby

23   Tom

24   Robert

25   Denise

Activity

A   sport

B   music

C   competition

D   dancing

E   food

F   exhibition

G   drinks

H   photography

You now have six minutes to write your answers on the answer sheet.

Test 4 SPEAKING

You are Candidate B. Answer the questions.

27–28

Do you like these different types of entertainment?

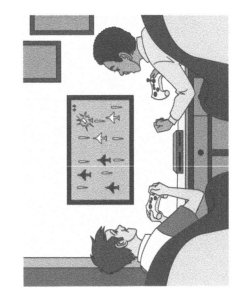

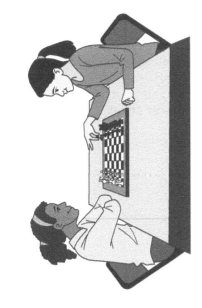

Audio scripts and Model answers on pages 167–223.

Test 5

TEST 5 READING AND WRITING

Part 1

Questions 1–6

For each question, choose the correct answer.

1

To: Students
From: Mrs Smith

Dear Students,

The temperature will be high 30s on Friday, so please bring a hat, sunglasses and some water on the trip.

Regards,
Mrs Smith

A Mrs Smith hopes the weather will be nice on the trip.

B Mrs Smith thinks it will be too hot to go on the trip.

C Mrs Smith wants students to remember things for the trip.

2

Feeling worried about exams?

Come and see me at break or lunchtime to chat.

Mrs Brown

A People who chat at lunchtime don't feel worried.

B Someone is worried and is asking for help.

C There is help for people who need it.

3

WARNING!

The lift isn't working. Please use the stairs next to the library.

A You don't need to use the lift to go to the library.

B You can only use the lift to go to the library.

C The lift isn't working in the library.

4

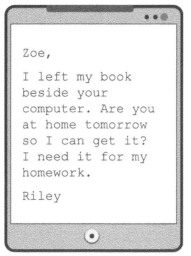

Zoe,

I left my book beside your computer. Are you at home tomorrow so I can get it? I need it for my homework.

Riley

A Zoe is asking Riley if he has found her book.

B Riley wants to get his book from Zoe.

C Zoe is asking Riley for help with her homework.

5

Jack,

Can you send me your address? You told me when I phoned you but I didn't write it down.

Thanks,

Matt

What should Jack do?

A Give Matt his address by email or text message.

B Phone Matt and tell him his address.

C Write down Matt's address.

6

A free drink with any meal or snack from our menu all day Wednesday.

A You can only get a drink if you choose a meal from the menu.

B You can get a free drink on any day.

C You have to buy food to get a free drink.

Part 2

Questions 7–13

For each question, choose the correct answer.

		Gemma	Mary	Ellie
7	Who thinks the food smells like some clothes?	A	B	C
8	Who has the food for breakfast?	A	B	C
9	Who says the name of the food doesn't describe what it is?	A	B	C
10	Whose talks about a person who helped a lot of people?	A	B	C
11	Who says you need a kind of fruit to make the food?	A	B	C
12	Who says that you can't find this food everywhere?	A	B	C
13	Who says the food looks very strange?	A	B	C

Unusual food

Gemma

I'm from Cornwall in the UK and we have an unusual dish here: Stargazey pie. It's made with fish, usually sardines, and we bake them whole in pastry with eggs and potatoes. It's traditional in a village called Mousehole. There's a story that long ago, people didn't have much money, and they were very hungry. A fisherman went out in a storm and caught enough fish for everyone in the village. The pie celebrates this brave fisherman. And the unusual part? The heads of the fish poke out from the pastry, gazing (or 'looking') at the stars!

Mary

An unusual type of food where I'm from, in Gloucestershire, is called Stinking Bishop. It's a type of cheese. It smells bad – like dirty socks! But it's delicious. When they make the cheese they wash it in juice from pears called Stinking Bishops. The pears get their name from Frederick Bishop, a farmer who grew the pears in the nineteenth century. You can't buy the cheese in supermarkets. It's special and you can only find it in a few shops in the UK.

Ellie

I'm from Wales and an unusual food here is called Laver bread. It isn't really bread at all. It's made from seaweed! To make Laver bread, you boil the seaweed for four hours and then mash it. It's a bright green colour and you can eat it with many things – with bread, meat, soup and fish. I like eating it in the morning before I go to school!

Part 3

Questions 14–18

For each question, choose the correct answer.

Crossing the English Channel on a flyboard™

by Victoria Hallam

Franky Zapata is an inventor and he is also the first person to cross the English Channel on a flyboard. He flew from Sangatte, near Calais in France at 6.17 a.m. on 4 August 2019 and landed in St Margaret's Bay in Dover, England. The 35.4-kilometre journey took exactly 22 minutes. Mr Zapata wore a special suit and a backpack. In the backpack there was fuel for the flyboard.

Mr Zapata travelled up to 170 kilometres per hour during the flight, but it wasn't easy. He needed to change to a different backpack during the flight because there wasn't enough fuel in the first backpack. The last time Mr Zapata tried to cross the English Channel he fell into the sea. Luckily, there was a boat waiting for him in the water. This time, three helicopters followed him across the sea.

'We made a machine three years ago ... and now we've crossed the Channel – it's crazy,' he told English journalists before he started crying with happiness.

Many people like Mr Zapata's machine. The French government have given him over £1.28 million to help him make more flyboards. So perhaps we will see more people flying on one in the future!

14 How did Mr Zapata cross the Channel?

    A He swam across it.

    B He flew across it.

    C He went by boat.

15 How far did he travel?

    A 170 kilometres

    B 22 kilometres

    C 35.4 kilometres

16 How did he not run out of fuel?

    A He used a second backpack.

    B A boat was waiting for him in the water.

    C He put more fuel in his backpack while he was flying.

17 How did he feel about crossing the Channel?

    A He was sad and worried about it.

    B He was happy and surprised.

    C He was crazy about it.

18 It is possible that in the future,

    A we will see more of Mr Zapata's machines.

    B everyone will travel on Mr Zapata's machines.

    C people will not travel by boat anymore.

Part 4

Questions 19–24

For each question, choose the correct answer.

Tim Peake

Tim Peake was the first British astronaut to live and work in space. The European Space Agency (ESA) **(19)** .... him to become an astronaut in 2009 and it took six years of training before he went into space in 2015. During his training, Tim **(20)** .... a week living underground and 12 days in a laboratory **(21)** .... the sea. He learnt about a lot about space and he also learnt to **(22)** .... Russian, the language used by the ESA. Living in space is difficult because there is zero gravity, so Tim had to learn how to stay **(23)** .... while he was floating around. Tim was in space for six **(24)** .... While he was there he did a spacewalk, and he was also the first astronaut to run a marathon in space!

19	**A** agreed	**B** decided	**C** chose
20	**A** spent	**B** took	**C** made
21	**A** through	**B** under	**C** over
22	**A** say	**B** talk	**C** speak
23	**A** safe	**B** tired	**C** hurt
24	**A** times	**B** months	**C** hours

Part 5

Questions 25–30

For each question, write the correct answer.
Write **one** word for each gap.

Example: | **0** | *to* |

EMAIL
From: Tina
To: Sofia

Dear Sofia,

I'm going **(0)** .... an art exhibition at the weekend. Do you want to come **(25)** .... me? The exhibition is for young artists in our area. There was an advertisement for a competition on the art gallery's website and I entered a painting I did at school. **(26)** .... you remember the one of the hills in the countryside at sunset? It won first prize! There will be **(27)** .... small party, too, and a journalist **(28)** .... the local newspaper will be there. **(29)** .... might get my picture in Sunday's newspaper! Let me know **(30)** .... you can come.

Speak soon,

Tina

Part 6

Question 31

You bought something new, but it has a problem.
Write a note about it to your English friend Lily.

In your note:

- tell Lily what you bought
- say what the problem is
- ask Lily for advice.

Write **25 words** or more.

Write the note on your answer sheet.

Part 7

Question 32

Look at the three pictures.
Write the story shown in the pictures.
Write **35 words** or more.

Write the story on your answer sheet.

TEST 5 LISTENING

Part 1

Questions 1–5

For each question, choose the correct answer.

---

1   Where will Helen meet David?

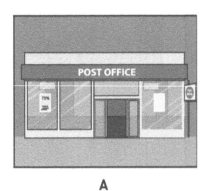

A

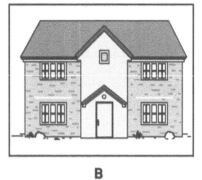

B

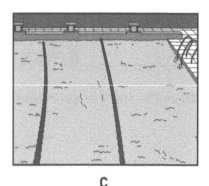

C

2   What time is the girl's new dentist's appointment?

A

B

C

3   Where can't the girl take photos?

A

B

C

4   How did Richard get to school today?

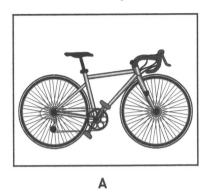

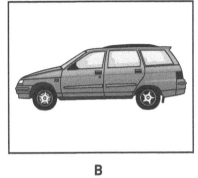

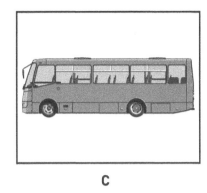

| A | B | C |

5   What will the weather be like this weekend?

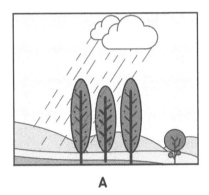

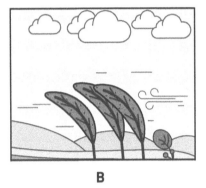

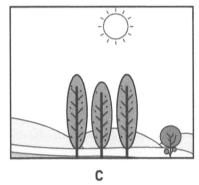

| A | B | C |

Part 2

30

Questions 6–10

For each question, write the correct answer in the gap. Write **one word** or **a number** or **a date** or **a time**.

You will hear a chef talking to a group of students about a baking club.

Baking Club

Club for:	Children aged 10 to 13
Teacher:	Mr **(6)** ....
Class times:	**(7)** .... a.m. to 2.30 p.m.
Small groups of:	**(8)** .... students
Ingredients needed:	Flour, butter **(9)** ...., eggs and sugar
Temperature of oven:	**(10)** ....°C

Part 3

31

Questions 11–15

For each question, choose the correct answer.

You will hear Brian talking to his friend Judy about going to the cinema.

11 How many people will go to the cinema?

  A two

  B three

  C four

12 Who doesn't want to see the action film?

  A Jack and Sylvia

  B Brian and Sylvia

  C Judy and Sylvia

13 The film about the zoo

  A has two men in it.

  B is very sad.

  C is a horror film.

14 Judy

  A doesn't want to dance or sing.

  B would like to watch a funny film.

  C hates films about animals.

15 Judy will meet the others

  A between quarter past three and four.

  B before three o'clock.

  C after half past two and before three.

Part 4

32

Questions 16–20

For each question, choose the correct answer.

---

16 You will hear a girl talking to her friend about her trip.
How does she feel now?

A tired

B excited

C bored

17 You will hear a boy talking to a friend on the phone.
Why is he excited?

A He's going to a concert.

B He's having a party.

C He's going to a party.

18 You will hear a mother talking to her son.
Where do they decide to put the desk?

A near the bed

B far from the bookcase

C in front of the window

19 You will hear a girl talking to her friend.
What does she need to buy?

A a T-shirt

B socks

C trainers

20 You will hear a girl talking to her teacher about school clubs.
What is she worried about?

A singing in front of people

B playing football

C having too many activities

Part 5

33

Questions 21–25

For each question, choose the correct answer.

You will hear Amber talking to Matt about sports.
What sport does each person do?

Example:

Matt ☐ H

People		Sport
21 Amber ☐		**A** cycling
22 Sue ☐		**B** basketball
23 Hannah ☐		**C** swimming
24 Paul ☐		**D** cricket
25 Jamie ☐		**E** skateboarding
		F hockey
		G sailing
		H badminton

You now have six minutes to write your answers on the answer sheet.

Test 5 SPEAKING

You are Candidate B. Answer the questions.

34–35

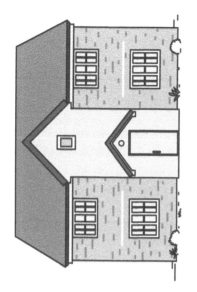

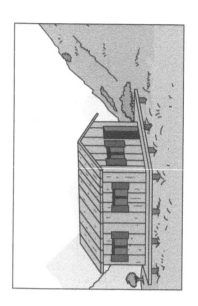

Do you like these different types of homes?

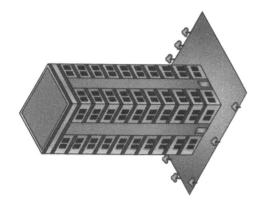

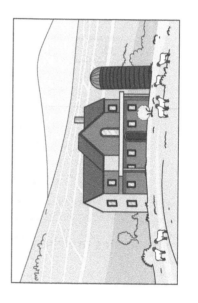

Audio scripts and Model answers on pages 167–223.

Test 6

TEST 6 READING AND WRITING

Part 1

Questions 1–6

For each question, choose the correct answer.

1

Did you see an accident outside here on Saturday 23rd March? Call 01923 393010

A If you had an accident here, call this number.

B If you saw an accident here on this date, call the number.

C If you have an accident here, call this number.

2

Please don't leave your swimming things in the changing rooms. Use the lockers.

A You must get dressed in the changing rooms.

B You mustn't leave the pool without your swimming things.

C You must put your swimming things in a locker.

3

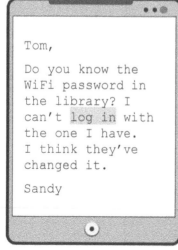

Tom,

Do you know the WiFi password in the library? I can't log in with the one I have. I think they've changed it.

Sandy

A Tom wants to know if they have changed the WiFi password.

B Tom doesn't know how to use the Internet.

C Sandy is not sure if Tom knows the WiFi password.

4

Lucia,

Let's work on our project on Saturday if you're free. You can come to my house and you can see my new laptop!

Emma

Why has Emma written this message?

A to offer Lucia help with her project

B to invite Lucia to her house

C to tell Lucia about her new laptop

5

Swimming team timetable
Training starts 5th September.
Check what group you're in with Mr Peters.

A Mr Peters will give you information about the timetable.

B If you want to join the swimming team, speak to Mr Peters.

C Mr Peters can give you information about the swimming team.

6

To all students!
Please note that the Study Room will be closed from 18th – 24th May for building work. Please use the library instead.

A The Study Room will be closed for a week, but the library will be open.

B You won't be able to study at school for a week.

C You can no longer study in the Study Room.

Part 2

Questions 7–13

For each question, choose the correct answer.

		Oliver	Evan	Michael
7	Who says that you probably don't get a good idea about a person's life online?	A	B	C
8	Who advises you not to let people know where to find you?	A	B	C
9	Who says that you shouldn't share information about yourself online?	A	B	C
10	Who suggests that you should be nice to other people online?	A	B	C
11	Who recommends asking for help if someone hurts your feelings online?	A	B	C
12	Who says that you should be careful online, even with people you like?	A	B	C
13	Who suggests a way of stopping people finding information about you on your phone?	A	B	C

Safety advice from teens

Oliver

Don't let people make you become someone you aren't. You may think you understand how the Internet works, but unexpected things can happen on the Internet. Posting photos or information online, even in emails, could become a problem for you in the future. People and friendships can change. And even people you think are your friends can use photos and information against you, especially if they stop being your friend.

Evan

Don't compare your own life to other people's lives. People usually post happy photos and stories online, but they don't often share their boring or unhappy times. Don't think they have a better life than you do. It is also a good idea not to say unkind things online; you should talk to people in the way that you would want them to talk to you. If someone is horrible to you, try not to get upset. Talk to a parent or teacher who can help.

Michael

Be clever when you use a smartphone. All the tips for keeping safe on a computer are the same for a phone. Be careful who you give your phone number to. Turn off the location setting on your phone so that it can't show where you are or where you have been. Keep your phone safe with a password. And make sure you know how to log into the iCloud or Android Find my Device so you can find or delete information from a lost or missing phone.

Part 3

Questions 14–18

For each question, choose the correct answer.

Feeling the music

by Kyle Meadows

Evelyn Glennie is one of the world's most famous musicians. However, she doesn't hear music like most of us. She feels it through her feet and body. Evelyn is deaf – she cannot hear. She feels the movement of sound through the floor and she can feel the rhythm and beat of the music.

Evelyn plays percussion instruments like the drums, and she performs solo at concerts around the world. When she was a child, she learned how to play musical instruments such as the harmonica and the piano. Then at the age of eight, she began to lose her hearing, but that didn't stop her love of music. She continued to play instruments while her hearing got worse, but she found that she could 'hear' notes in her feet and body.

Evelyn decided to learn the drums after she saw a friend playing them. At the age of 16, she started studying at a music college in England and she graduated three years later. At 23, she won her first Grammy award. She is the first person in musical history to have a career as a solo percussion player.

Evelyn performs and practises with bare feet; she can't feel the music well if she wears shoes. She also teaches other musicians, and her YouTube videos teach people how to listen. She hopes that people will live better if they learn to listen better. She also collects percussion instruments and has more than 2,000 drums and other instruments. Evelyn now works with orchestras all around the world.

14 How is Evelyn different from other musicians?

    A She doesn't listen to the same kind of music.

    B She doesn't use her ears to experience music.

    C She moves differently from other musicians.

15 When Evelyn was eight years old,

    A she stopped listening to music.

    B she didn't play the piano.

    C she learnt to do something.

16 Before Evelyn, no other person with hearing problems

    A had a career playing percussion music at concerts.

    B won an important award for music at the age of 23.

    C could go to college to study music.

17 How does Evelyn practise?

    A with other musicians

    B with other students

    C with no shoes on

18 Evelyn thinks that

    A if you listen to music better, your life will also improve.

    B collecting musical instruments has made her a better musician.

    C her online videos will help people enjoy her music more.

Part 4

Questions 19–24

For each question, choose the correct answer.

Mya-Rose Craig

Mya-Rose Craig, also **(19)** .... as Birdgirl, is a British bird expert who travels around the world to see rare birds. Her aim is to see 5,400 different **(20)** .... of birds – half of the world's species.

Mya-Rose spends most of her free time **(21)** .... birds. She writes about them on social media and her blog. At the weekend she goes birdwatching. She loves organising weekend nature camps and meeting other young people who are **(22)** .... in nature. She loves nature and wildlife, and she believes that birds are very special. Mya-Rose is right: these amazing animals can fly **(23)** .... the air.

Mya-Rose wants **(24)** .... to enjoy nature. She thinks that young people should go outside more and enjoy the wildlife because our planet needs them.

19	**A** called	**B** known	**C** spoken
20	**A** groups	**B** members	**C** kinds
21	**A** looking for	**B** looking after	**C** looking out
22	**A** worried	**B** interested	**C** excited
23	**A** through	**B** along	**C** across
24	**A** anyone	**B** someone	**C** everyone

Part 5

Questions 25–30

For each question, write the correct answer.
Write **one** word for each gap.

Example: | **0** | *be* |

EMAIL	
From:	Hugo
To:	Lucia

What will the temperature **(0)** .... like at the weekend? Do you think it will rain again **(25)** .... will it be sunny? We could go swimming at the outdoor pool **(26)** .... it's warm enough. I **(27)** .... a piano lesson in the morning, but we could meet in the afternoon. My dad is working **(28)** .... Saturday so I'll come by bike. Would it be OK if my younger brother comes too? My mum says I have to look after **(29)** .... for a few hours while she **(30)** .... shopping. Let me know what you think.

See you soon!

Part 6

Question 31

Your English friend Ethan is coming to visit you for a few days.
Write an email to Ethan.

In your email:

- ask Ethan when his flight arrives
- ask what food Ethan likes and dislikes
- say what activities you can do.

Write **25 words** or more.

Write the email on your answer sheet.

Part 7

Questions 32

Look at the three pictures.
Write the story shown in the pictures.
Write **35 words** or more.

Write the story on your answer sheet.

TEST 6 LISTENING

Part 1

Questions 1–5

For each question, choose the correct answer.

---

1   Where did the girl's father see the notebook?

A

B

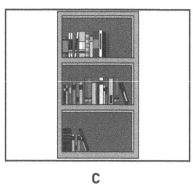

C

2   Where did the boy find out about the exhibition?

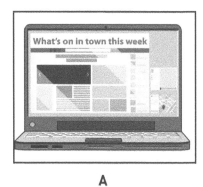

A

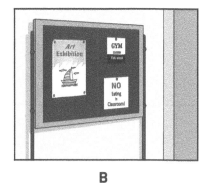

B

C

3   What does Cathy's brother look like?

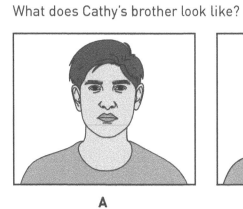

A

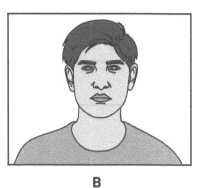

B

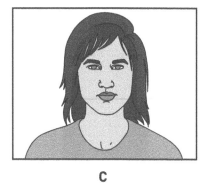

C

4 What would the woman like help with?

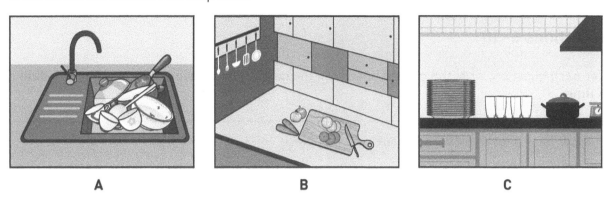

A   B   C

5 What time is the girl's doctor's appointment?

A   B   C

Part 2

37

Questions 6–10

For each question, write the correct answer in the gap. Write **one word** or **a number** or **a date** or **a time**.

You will hear a teacher talking about a special place.

Harbin, China **The Ice City**	
Season:	Winter
Number of builders:	**(6)** ....
Ice from:	A large **(7)** ....
Average temperature:	**(8)** .... °C below zero
Number of visitors:	over **(9)** .... million
Opening date:	**(10)** .... January

Part 3

38

Questions 11–15

For each question, choose the correct answer.

You will hear Cara talking to her friend Tina about a summer holiday.

11 Which month is Tina able to go on the trip?

    A June

    B July

    C August

12 Cara learnt about the adventure holiday from

    A a website.

    B school.

    C her friend.

13 What is Cara interested in doing on holiday?

    A water sports

    B climbing

    C hiking and cooking

14 How much is the trip?

    A £285

    B £270

    C £385

15 The girls will need to pay extra for

    A transport.

    B accommodation.

    C meals.

Part 4

Questions 16–20

For each question, choose the correct answer.

___

16 You will hear a man talking on the phone.
What is he recommending?

A a person

B a place to live

C a college

17 You will hear a boy talking to a shop assistant.
Why is he upset?

A His new camera takes bad photos.

B He can't use his new camera.

C His broke his new camera.

18 You will hear a girl talking to her friend on the phone.
What does she need to do?

A fill in a form

B print a form

C go to the school office

19 You will hear two friends talking about holidays.
Where did Marcus go?

A Scotland

B Japan

C Australia

20 You will hear two friends talking about the weekend.
Who did the girl visit?

A her grandfather

B her cousin

C her aunt

Part 5

40

Questions 21–25

For each question, choose the correct answer.

You will hear Emily talking to her friend Duncan about visiting her family in Canada. What gift has Emily's mum bought for each person?

Example:

Uncle Zac | E |

People

21	Uncle Jim
22	Aunt Maisie
23	Simon
24	Tamsin
25	Granny

Gifts

A jewellery

B digital radio

C camera

D handbag

E football shirt

F headphones

G book

H gloves

You now have six minutes to write your answers on the answer sheet.

Test 6 SPEAKING

You are Candidate B. Answer the questions.

41–42

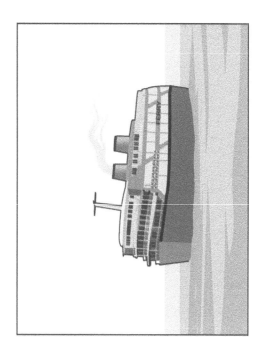

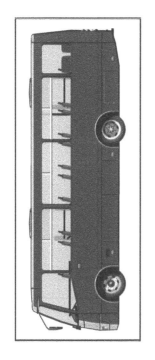

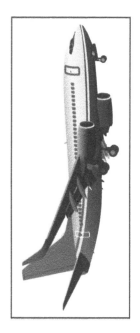

Do you like these different ways to travel?

Audio scripts and Model answers on pages 167–223.

Test 7

TEST 7 READING AND WRITING

Part 1

Questions 1–6

For each question, choose the correct answer.

1

> **Stay healthy!**
>
> - Eat well
> - Exercise often
> - Get lots of sleep

A Find more information about how to stay healthy.

B Follow these rules to live well.

C Help others to stay healthy.

2

> **Please leave the camping area how you found it.**
>
> **Take all rubbish when you leave.**

A Put all your rubbish in one area.

B People can't leave at the area if they leave their rubbish there.

C Don't leave the area and leave your rubbish there.

3

> Hi Paul,
>
> I'm online, booking the concert tickets. Do you want to stand near the stage or have a seat? Let me know!
>
> Ben

What does Paul need to do?

A Decide where he would like to be at the concert.

B Buy the concert tickets online.

C Meet Ben near the stage at the concert.

4

To: Kim
From: Sarah
Hi Kim,
You left your tennis kit at my house.
Do you want me to bring it to you at school tomorrow?
Sarah

A Kim forgot to bring her tennis kit to school.

B Sarah wants to know what to do with Kim's tennis kit.

C Sarah reminds Kim to bring her tennis kit tomorrow.

5

School party

18th December
7–10 p.m.
Write your name if you
can come.

A Students must come to the party.

B Students must say if they are going to the party.

C Students must write about the party.

6

Need help quickly?

Laptop and mobile phone repair

Call Ben on 01238 987654

A Ben needs help with his laptop and mobile phone.

B If you need a new laptop, call Ben.

C You can speak to Ben if you have problems with your laptop.

Part 2

Questions 7–13

For each question, choose the correct answer.

		Jian	Daniel	Ahmed
7	Who describes a camp that isn't like usual summer camps?	A	B	C
8	Who says the camp offers water sports?	A	B	C
9	Who doesn't talk about language skills?	A	B	C
10	Who says the camp gives people something for learning things at the camp?	A	B	C
11	Who says the camp offers people a chance to see different parts of the country?	A	B	C
12	Who liked a place where he slept?	A	B	C
13	Who took part in a long-distance challenge at the camp?	A	B	C

International summer camp recommendations

Jian

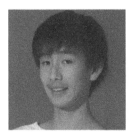

The Summer River Camp in France is fantastic. You can do some exciting activities, like rock climbing and canoeing. At the end of your stay, you take part in a 30-kilometre canoe trip down the river and spend the night at a campsite in the forest. There are tents with camp beds, so you don't sleep on the hard ground. The camp is also great if you want to speak French better because a lot of kids from the local area go to the camp.

Daniel

I went to Survival Camp in Germany last year and it was amazing! The camp is in a national park and it is the best outdoor adventure. You go into the forest and learn how to live there. You learn how to make fires, find food and make a safe and dry place to sleep. At the end of the week, each person gets a medal that shows they are now real survivors who can live in the wild if they have to. It's fantastic if you like adventures.

Ahmed

If you want something different, try the Mandarin Camp in China. It's great if you want to enjoy China's amazing culture and learn Chinese. The teachers are friendly and make learning fun. There are lots of different activities, for example, calligraphy and cartoon making, and there are trips to local museums. There's even a trip to the Great Wall of China! You'll have free time, so you can make friends with the other kids at the camp.

Part 3

Questions 14–18

For each question, choose the correct answer.

Tips to stop feeling tired at school

by Jane Carew

Sleep is very important. While we are resting, our brain processes what we have done and seen all day, and our body repairs itself. Scientists have found that sleeping is necessary for our physical and mental health. Many people don't sleep enough, and this isn't good for us. If we don't sleep enough, we have less energy and we lose the ability to think clearly.

A good night's sleep starts with what you do during the day. It is harder to get to sleep at night if you still have lots of energy, so you should exercise daily. Try going for a walk or a run, and do some sport as often as you can.

It is hard to sleep when your brain is working. Try not to do your homework at the last minute, don't exercise late in the day and don't drink anything with lots of sugar. If you find it difficult to calm down at night, take a cool shower, read or drink a glass of water slowly.

It can be hard to stick to a routine, but your body will thank you for it: try to go to bed at the same time each night and wake up at the same time each morning.

Many of us like to relax by playing computer games, going on social media or checking for text messages. These are great ways to relax during the day, but in the hour before you go to bed put your electronic gadgets away. The lights from screens can keep us awake.

14 What does the text say about sleep?

    A It isn't good for us to sleep for too many hours.

    B Sleeping changes how we think and feel.

    C If you are not well, you should sleep more.

15 What can stop you from sleeping at night?

    A if you haven't exercised enough that day

    B if you walk or run during the day

    C if you are a person with lots of energy

16 It can be difficult to sleep if

    A you have a shower before bedtime.

    B you drink too much water in the evening.

    C you study late at night.

17 You should try to

    A sleep the same number of hours each night.

    B go to bed only when you are tired.

    C go to sleep early and wake up early.

18 We should not look at our phones

    A a few hours before bedtime.

    B during the day.

    C right before bedtime.

Part 4

Questions 19–24

For each question, choose the correct answer.

Madame Tussauds

Madame Tussauds is a famous museum in London, where visitors can see lifelike wax statues of famous people. The first Madame Tussauds museum opened over 200 years ago. It was started by Madame Marie Tussauds, who was an art **(19)** .... in France. She made wax masks of **(20)** .... people. Today, the artists who work at Madame Tussauds usually **(21)** .... about four months to make a wax statue. First, they **(22)** .... a lot of photographs of a person because they help them in their work. The artists use a lot of wax to make a statue and the head alone can **(23)** .... about five kilograms. Then they add hair to the statue's head. This **(24)** .... can take about 140 hours to finish. After that, they paint the statue's face and, finally, they dress it.

19	**A** worker		**B** person		**C** teacher
20	**A** important		**B** favourite		**C** interested
21	**A** try		**B** need		**C** do
22	**A** put		**B** make		**C** take
23	**A** weigh		**B** cost		**C** take
24	**A** way		**B** step		**C** plan

Part 5

Questions 25–30

For each question, write the correct answer.
Write **one** word for each gap.

Example: | 0 | *but* |

> **EMAIL**
>
> From: | Sofie
> To: | Jade
>
> Dear Jade,
>
> I'm really sorry, **(0)** .... I won't be able to come to your party today. I have a stomachache and I'm **(25)** .... feeling well. I probably caught something from my sister. She was sick yesterday **(26)** .... she didn't go to school. She was in bed all day. I have **(27)** .... high temperature and I feel tired, too. I'm sad because I was really looking forward to your party! I bought a present **(28)** .... you and I'll give it to you next week at school **(29)** .... I'm feeling better again. I hope **(30)** .... enjoy the party.
>
> Eat a piece of cake for me!
> Sofie

Part 6

Question 31

You arranged a time to meet your English friend Zoe about the school study club. Write an email to Zoe.

In your email:

- tell Zoe what the study club is for
- say when the members of the club meet
- say where in the school the club meets.

Write **25 words** or more.

Write the email on your answer sheet.

Part 7

Question 32

Look at the three pictures.
Write the story shown in the pictures.
Write **35 words** or more.

Write the story on your answer sheet.

TEST 7 LISTENING

Part 1

43

Questions 1–5

For each question, choose the correct answer.

---

1 Where is the ticket machine?

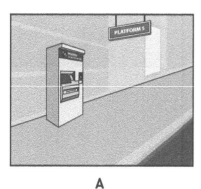

A   B   C

2 Where are the two friends going?

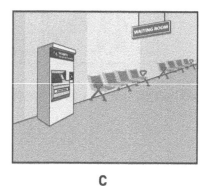

A   B   C

3 How long will the woman stay at the hotel?

A   B   C

4   Where is the library?

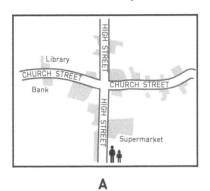

A

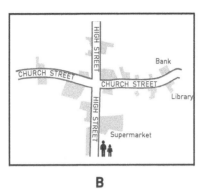

B

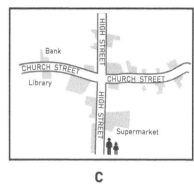

C

5   What will they buy?

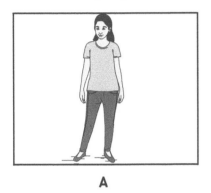

A

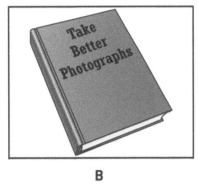

B

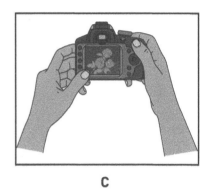

C

Part 2

Questions 6–10

For each question, write the correct answer in the gap. Write **one word** or **a number** or **a date** or **a time**.

You will hear a teacher talking to a group of students about a school event.

Environment action

Name:	The Great School Clean-up
Date:	Friday **(6)** .... April
Cleaning:	The park, the **(7)** ...., the town centre and the forest
Duration:	**(8)** .... hours
Wear:	**(9)** .... clothes and shoes, thick gloves
The school will give:	plastic **(10)** .... and litter pickers

Part 3

45

Questions 11–15

For each question, choose the correct answer.

You will hear Sofia talking to her friend, Oliver, about their school project.

11 One thing they need to find out is

    A if any students are learning other languages.

    B how well students speak other languages.

    C why some students are learning other languages.

12 Why can't they speak to everyone in the school?

    A Not everyone wants to answer questions.

    B They don't know everyone.

    C They don't have enough time.

13 Oliver suggests that they get information

    A at the school office.

    B in the library.

    C from their teacher.

14 On his first day at the school, Oliver

    A had to speak another language.

    B answered some questions.

    C completed a form for everyone in his class.

15 What does Sofia decide to do?

    A see Mrs Davis immediately

    B arrange to see Mrs Davis

    C phone Mrs Davis after class

Part 4

46

Questions 16–20

For each question, choose the correct answer.

---

16 You will hear a boy talking on the phone.
What is he planning to do?

    A go to a sports match

    B go to the cinema

    C go to a festival

17 You will hear a girl talking to her friend about food.
What can't she eat?

    A salad

    B chicken

    C mushrooms

18 You will hear a boy talking to his friend.
What is he worried about?

    A finding the place

    B his interview

    C getting on the bus

19 You will hear a girl talking to her friend.
Why didn't she go to the swimming pool?

    A She wasn't feeling well.

    B She was having dinner.

    C She was at the library.

20 You will hear two friends talking about a camping trip.
What did the girl see?

    A colourful trees

    B colourful fields

    C colourful flowers

Part 5

Questions 21–25

For each question, choose the correct answer.

You will hear Harry talking to Eleanor about her trip.
What was the weather like on each day?

Example:

0   Monday | F |

Days		**Weather**
21 Tuesday	☐	**A** sunny
22 Wednesday	☐	**B** stormy
23 Thursday	☐	**C** foggy
24 Friday	☐	**D** hot
25 Saturday	☐	**E** snowy
		F cloudy
		G windy
		H cold

You now have six minutes to write your answers on the answer sheet.

Test 7 SPEAKING

You are Candidate B. Answer the questions.

48–49

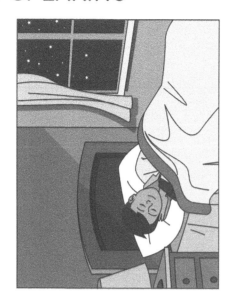

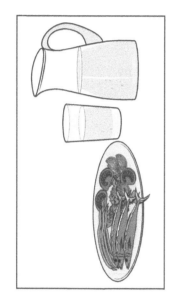

Do you like these different ways to stay healthy?

Audio scripts and Model answers on pages 167–223.

Test 8

TEST 8 READING AND WRITING

Part 1

Questions 1–6

For each question, choose the correct answer.

1

> **Back to school supplies**
>
> **Books, pencils, rulers**
>
> **All half price until Friday 10th.**

A You pay less for school things until Friday.

B School things cost less after Friday.

C Students need to bring their things to school on Friday.

2

> Join our band!
>
> Can you sing or play an instrument?
>
> Meeting in Music Room, lunchtime

A You need to be able to sing to join the band.

B You can find out about joining the band at lunchtime.

C There will be music lessons at lunchtime.

3

> **School lunch menu: Monday 11th October**
>
> - Salad
> - Chicken, potatoes, vegetables
> - Fruit

A The lunch menu is the same every day.

B This is the food you can eat on this day.

C You can choose only one thing on the menu.

4

Why did Emily's mum write the message?

A to check if Emily is at home

B to remind Emily about photography club

C to tell Emily who is taking her to photography club

5

A José didn't know that Wei lost his notes.

B José must call Wei about the maths lesson.

C José's dad wants him to find Wei's maths notes.

6

To: Louise
From: Hilary
Louise, Wasn't the exam awful?! Let's meet for pizza on Saturday and talk about it. Lisa says she can come too. Are you free? Hilary

A Hilary wants to talk to Lisa about the exam.

B Hilary and Louise had the same exam.

C Louise knows that Lisa can meet her and Hilary on Saturday.

Part 2

Questions 7–13

For each question, choose the correct answer.

		Noor	Janice	Chloe
7	Who started being healthier after reading about something?	A	B	C
8	Who has made the biggest change in her life?	A	B	C
9	Who learnt about the right food because of something she did at school?	A	B	C
10	Who makes sure she exercises a lot every week?	A	B	C
11	Who recommends not eating a lot of fast food?	A	B	C
12	Who isn't very active now but knows she should exercise more?	A	B	C
13	Who started doing an activity a short time ago that will help her become healthier?	A	B	C

Healthy teens

Noor

Last month my class did a project about health and I learnt some useful information. We should eat at least seven portions of fruit and vegetables a day as well as meat and fish, eggs, milk and cheese. It's fine to eat things like burgers and pizza sometimes, but too many could make us overweight and feel unwell. Exercise is also important. I took up yoga last week. It's great for your body and a great way to relax.

Janice

I came across a magazine about keeping healthy while I was waiting at the dentist's. A healthy diet is important for young people because we are still growing. The right diet keeps both our brain and body strong. Now I try to have food like fruit, vegetables, milk, fish and eggs every day, and I drink lots of water. I don't exercise a lot but now I know it's important. I'm going to start exercising regularly from Monday.

Chloe

I started eating more healthily last year. I spent too much time playing video games and I didn't go outside to exercise. I put on weight and started to feel tired. My friend suggested I start walking for half an hour each day. Well, it was a miracle cure! I became fitter and I even started to run. I lost weight, and the exercise gave me more energy. Now I run three times a week, I walk the dog every evening and I eat healthy foods. It's important to look after yourself!

Part 3

Questions 14–18

For each question, choose the correct answer.

Back to school ... and relax!

by Robbie Nicholson

School seemed easier when you were younger. Now things are different; there is lots more studying and lots of planning for the future. You can soon start feeling stressed, so here are some things you can do to feel more relaxed.

Plan ahead. Get a wall calendar or personal planner. Mark the dates of tests and exams on it. Note the dates when you have to give in projects, essays and other homework. List any other activities you have, like basketball practice. When your calendar starts to get full, say no to other activities until things calm down.

Stay ahead. If you feel that you are falling behind with your work and start becoming worried, let your teachers know. Almost all students have problems with something at school, so if you are having difficulty with a subject or a project, ask your teacher for help. If you take a few minutes to deal with the problem right away, you will save time and worry later.

Take notes. If you take notes and read them before class begins or while you are studying for an exam, you can ask a teacher to explain anything you don't understand. It can also be helpful to check that you have understood your notes with a friend after class, but make sure your friend really understands the lesson! Learning good note-taking skills in school will also help you do well at university, when good lecture notes are very important if you want to get good marks.

14 What does the writer say can be a reason for stress?

    A not knowing what to do in the future

    B having many things to do at school

    C feeling unhappy about getting older

15 It is a good idea to use a calendar because

    A it helps you do your homework.

    B it helps you save time during the week.

    C it stops you from doing too much.

16 If you are finding lessons difficult,

    A you shouldn't try to deal with the problem by yourself.

    B you must ask your teachers for extra homework.

    C you can study with students who have the same problem.

17 Students should look at their notes

    A with a teacher.

    B during an exam.

    C before class.

18 Good note-taking skills will help you

    A get into a good university.

    B write good lectures.

    C in the future.

Part 4

Questions 19–24

For each question, choose the correct answer.

The Amazon River

The Amazon River begins in the Andes Mountains and **(19)** .... more than 6,000 kilometres to the Atlantic Ocean. It is the second longest river in the world. Most of the river's water comes from rain. During the wet **(20)** .... , there is so much water in the river that it is 190 kilometres **(21)** .... near the sea. The river goes mainly **(22)** .... rainforests, not cities. That is why there are no **(23)** .... that go across it. More than half of the river is in Brazil, in the world's largest rainforest. The Amazon rainforest has the **(24)** .... number of plant and animal species on Earth – more than 40,000 different kinds of plants and about 3,000 kinds of fish – and there are still many more animals and plants for us to discover.

19	**A** travels	**B** moves	**C** goes
20	**A** age	**B** date	**C** season
21	**A** strong	**B** wide	**C** deep
22	**A** in	**B** on	**C** through
23	**A** bridges	**B** buildings	**C** corners
24	**A** greatest	**B** best	**C** least

Part 5

Questions 25–30

For each question, write the correct answer.
Write **one** word for each gap.

Example: | 0 | *for* |

> **EMAIL**
>
> From: Emilia
>
> To: Alex
>
> Hi Alex,
>
> Are you ready **(0)** .... the camping trip? We have to be **(25)** .... school at 6 a.m. tomorrow morning. Mum told me to take a warm jacket with me because **(26)** .... may be cold. I'm really excited about the trip. It's **(27)** .... to be a lot of fun. I've **(28)** .... been camping before.
>
> Are you taking your swimming costume? Mrs Smith says we will be near **(29)** .... lake, but I think it will be **(30)** .... cold to go swimming. Oh, and I've packed lots of snacks, too!

Part 6

Question 31

Your want to invite your English friend Neil to your house this weekend.
Write an email to Neil.

In your email:

- invite Neil to your house this weekend
- say what day and time Neil could come
- tell Neil what you can do at your house.

Write **25 words** or more.

Write the email on your answer sheet.

Part 7

Question 32

Look at the three pictures.
Write the story shown in the pictures.
Write **35 words** or more.

Write the story on your answer sheet.

TEST 8 LISTENING

Part 1

Questions 1–5

For each question, choose the correct answer.

---

1 What time is Derek's train?

A

B

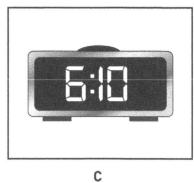

C

2 How will they get to the dentist's office?

A

B

C

3 What does the boy have to buy?

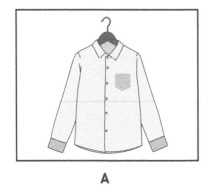

A

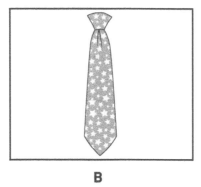

B

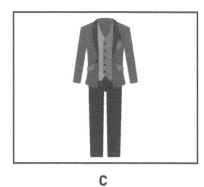

C

4 What do they need from the supermarket?

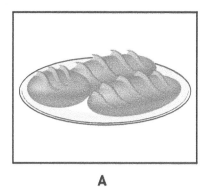 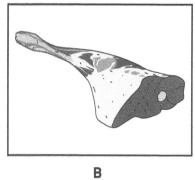 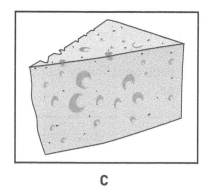

| A | B | C |

5 What does Rachel's mother suggest?

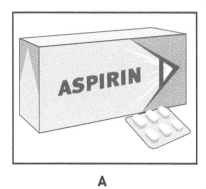  

| A | B | C |

Part 2

51

Questions 6–10

For each question, write the correct answer in the gap. Write **one word** or **a number** or **a date** or **a time**.

You will hear a student giving a talk about the world's tallest building.

A problem with the Burj Khalifa, the world's tallest building

Height:	800 metres
Problem:	The windows get **(6)** ....
Number of people in the team:	**(7)** ....
Number of windows:	**(8)** ....
The time the job takes:	**(9)** .... months
Type of job:	dangerous but **(10)** ....

Part 3

52

Questions 11–15

For each question, choose the correct answer.

___

You will hear Sam talking to her friend Ivan about joining a gym.

11 The gym is next to the

    A park.

    B library.

    C department store.

12 Sam says the gym is

    A not very big.

    B often busy.

    C not expensive.

13 Ivan suggests it is better to pay for the gym

    A every time you go.

    B every month.

    C once a year.

14 What else does the gym have?

    A a café and a juice bar

    B a swimming pool and a café

    C a juice bar and a swimming pool

15 What does Ivan think?

    A Sam does a lot of sport.

    B Sam should join the gym.

    C She has a lot of free time.

Part 4

53

Questions 16–20

For each question, choose the correct answer.

---

16 You will hear two friends talking about a pair of sunglasses.
What doesn't the girl like about them?

   A the shape

   B the colour

   C the size

17 You will hear a boy talking about his journey to school this morning.
How did he get there?

   A He walked.

   B He came by bus.

   C He came by car.

18 You will hear a girl talking to her friend about a new mobile phone.
Why did she buy it?

   A She needed a better camera.

   B Her old phone stopped working.

   C It wasn't expensive.

19 You will hear a boy talking to his friend about an accident.
What happened?

   A He broke his finger.

   B He cut his finger.

   C He broke his arm.

20 You will hear a girl talking to her friend about a party.
What does she need help with?

   A putting things on the table

   B preparing the food

   C decorating the place

Part 5

54

Questions 21–25

For each question, choose the correct answer.

You will hear Bella talking to a school advisor about different subjects.
What does each person suggest that she study at university?

Example:

Bella   ┃ **E** ┃

People		**Subjects**
21 Dad	☐	**A** art
22 Mum	☐	**B** mathematics
23 brother	☐	**C** teaching
24 manager	☐	**D** medicine
25 grandfather	☐	**E** history
		F music
		G geography
		H science

You now have six minutes to write your answers on the answer sheet.

Test 8 SPEAKING

You are Candidate B. Answer the questions.

55–56

Do you like these different types of weather?

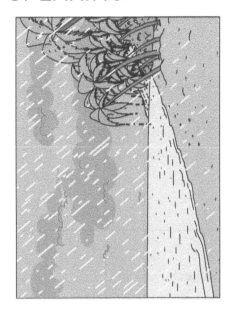

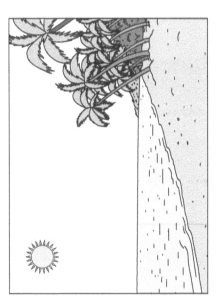

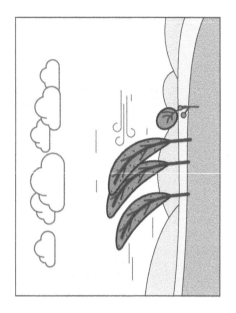

Audio scripts and Model answers on pages 167–223.

Mini-dictionary

 Here are some of the more difficult words from the practice tests. Definitions and examples are from *Collins COBUILD* Dictionaries.

TEST 1

blow /bləʊ/ **(blows, blowing, blowed)** VERB to send air from your mouth into an object so that it makes a sound • *When the referee blows his whistle, the game begins.*

bone /bəʊn/ **(bones)** NOUN one of the hard white parts inside your body • *Many passengers suffered broken bones in the accident.*

cave /keɪv/ **(caves)** NOUN a large hole in the side of a hill or under the ground • *They discovered a cave more than 1,000 feet deep.*

climate change /ˈklaɪmət ˌtʃeɪndʒ/ NOUN changes in the earth's climate, especially the fact that it is getting warmer because of high levels of certain gases • *Species are becoming extinct because of climate change.*

faraway /fɑːrəˈweɪ/ ADJECTIVE used when talking about something that is a long way from someone or something • *They have just returned from faraway places.*

flute /fluːt/ **(flutes)** NOUN a musical instrument that you hold sideways to your mouth and play by blowing • *I started playing the flute in primary school.*

friendship /ˈfrendʃɪp/ **(friendships)** NOUN a relationship between two or more friends • *Their friendship has lasted more than sixty years.*

hole /həʊl/ **(holes)** NOUN an opening or tear in something • *I've got a hole in my jeans.*

muddy /ˈmʌdi/ ADJECTIVE covered with mud • *Philip left his muddy boots at the kitchen door.*

note /nəʊt/ **(notes)** NOUN one particular sound, or a symbol that represents this sound • *She has a deep voice and can't sing high notes.*

planet /ˈplænɪt/ **(planets)** NOUN a large, round object in space that moves around a star. The Earth is a planet. • *We study the planets in the solar system.*

public /ˈpʌblɪk/ NOUN **The public** are people in general, or everyone. • *The exhibition is open to the public from tomorrow.*

queue /kjuː/ **(queues, queuing, queued)** VERB If a line of people or vehicles **queue**, they wait for something. • *I had to queue for quite a while.*

sandal /ˈsændəl/ **(sandals)** NOUN a light shoe that you wear in warm weather • *He put on a pair of old sandals.*

scientist /ˈsaɪəntɪst/ **(scientists)** NOUN someone whose job is to teach or do research in science • *Scientists have discovered a new gene.*

solve /sɒlv/ **(solves, solving, solved)** VERB to find an answer to a problem or a question • *They have not solved the problem of unemployment.*

wind instrument /ˈwɪnd ˌɪnstrəmənt/ **(wind instruments)** NOUN any musical instrument that you blow into to produce sounds • *Henry was keen to learn to play a wind instrument.*

TEST 2

afterwards /ˈɑːftəwʊdz/ ADVERB in the time after a particular event or time that you have already mentioned • *Shortly afterwards, the police arrived.*

carry on /ˈkæri ɒn/ **(carries on, carrying on, carried on)** PHRASAL VERB to continue to do something • *The teacher carried on talking.*

changing room /ˈtʃeɪndʒɪŋ ˌruːm/ **(changing rooms)** NOUN a room in a sports centre where you can change your clothes and usually have a shower • *I ran and hid in the changing room.*

comment /ˈkɒment/ **(comments)** NOUN an opinion about something • *It is difficult to make a comment about the situation.*

create /kriˈeɪt/ **(creates, creating, created)** VERB to make something happen • *It's great for a group of schoolchildren to create a show like this.*

damaged /dæmɪdʒd/ ADJECTIVE broken or harmed • *A damaged car sat at the side of the road.*

judge /dʒʌdʒ/ **(judges)** NOUN a person who decides who will be the winner of a competition • *A panel of judges will choose the winner.*

lab /læb/ **(labs)** NOUN a building or a room where scientific work is done. Lab is short for 'laboratory'. • *He works in a research lab at the university.*

makeover /ˈmeɪkoʊvə/ **(makeovers)** NOUN If a person or thing is given a **makeover**, their appearance is improved. • *She had a makeover at a beauty salon as a birthday gift.*

marathon /ˈmærəθən/ **(marathons)** NOUN a race in which people run a distance of 26 miles (= about 42 km) • *He is running in his first marathon next weekend.*

publish /ˈpʌblɪʃ/ **(publishes, publishing, published)** VERB to prepare and print copies of a book, a magazine or a newspaper • *HarperCollins will publish his new novel on March 4.*

set up /set ʌp/ **(sets up, setting up, set up)** PHRASAL VERB to start or arrange something • *He plans to set up his own business.*

slip /slɪp/ **(slips, slipping, slipped)** VERB to accidentally slide and fall • *He slipped on the wet grass.*

training /ˈtreɪnɪŋ/ NOUN preparation for a sports event • *He keeps fit through exercise and training.*

TEST 3

ancient /ˈeɪnʃənt/ ADJECTIVE very old, or from a long time ago • *ancient Scottish traditions*

archaeologist /ˌɑːkiˈɒlədʒɪst/ **(archaeologists)** NOUN someone who studies the past by examining the things that remain, such as buildings and tools • *Archaeologists discovered buildings from an ancient culture in Mexico City.*

community /kəˈmjuːnɪti/ **(communities)** NOUN a group of people who live in a particular area • *When you live in a small community, everyone knows you.*

create /kriˈeɪt/ **(creates, creating, created)** VERB to make something • *It's great for a group of schoolchildren to create a show like this.*

elderly /ˈeldəli/ ADJECTIVE used as a polite way of saying that someone is old • *An elderly couple lived in the house next door.*

stone /stəʊn/ **(stones)** NOUN a hard solid substance that is found in the ground and is often used for building • *The room had a stone floor.*

structure /ˈstrʌktʃə/ **(structures)** NOUN something that has been built • *This modern brick and glass structure was built in 1905.*

TEST 4

blind /blaɪnd/ ADJECTIVE unable to see • *My grandfather is going blind.*

classify /ˈklæsɪfaɪ/ **(classifies, classifying, classified)** VERB to divide things into groups or types • *Vitamins can be classified into two categories.*

code /kəʊd/ **(codes)** NOUN a way to replace words with other words or symbols • *They sent messages using codes.*

designer /dɪˈzaɪnə/ **(designers)** NOUN a person whose job is to design things by making drawings of them • *Caroline is a fashion designer.*

environment /ɪnˈvaɪərənmənt/ **(environments)** NOUN the natural world of land, the seas, the air, plants and animals • *Please respect the environment by recycling.*

exchange programme /ɪksˈtʃeɪndʒ ˌprəʊɡræm/ **(exchange programmes)** NOUN An **exchange programme** is when people from different countries visit each other's country. • *They went on an exchange programme to Spain.*

gamer /ˈɡeɪmə/ **(gamers)** NOUN someone who plays computer games • *They chat and argue with other gamers.*

ground /ɡraʊnd/ NOUN the surface of the Earth or the floor of a room • *He fell to the ground.*

high street /ˈhaɪ ˌstriːt/ **(high streets)** NOUN the main street where most of the shops and banks are • *Vegetarian restaurants are now found on every high street.*

ingredient /ɪnˈɡriːdiənt/ **(ingredients)** NOUN one of the things that you use to make something, especially when you are cooking • *Mix together all the ingredients.*

invent /ɪnˈvent/ **(invents, inventing, invented)** VERB to be the first person to think of something or to make it • *The ballpoint pen was invented by the Hungarian, Laszlo Biro.*

ordinary /'ɔ:dɪnri/ ADJECTIVE normal and not special or different • *These are just ordinary people living ordinary lives.*

second-hand /'sekənd,hænd/ ADJECTIVE already used by another person; not new • *They could just afford a second-hand car.*

sight /saɪt/ NOUN the ability to see • *Grandpa has lost the sight in his right eye.*

similar /'sɪmɪlə/ ADJECTIVE the same in some ways but not in every way • *Nowadays, cars all look very similar.*

TEST 5

astronaut /'æstrənɔ:t/ (astronauts) NOUN a person who is trained for travelling in space • *I was five when I first started thinking about being an astronaut.*

celebrate /'selɪˌbreɪt/ (celebrates, celebrating, celebrated) VERB If you **celebrate** someone, you think a lot of them and praise them. • *Let's celebrate this great athlete.*

comedy /'kɒmədi/ (comedies) NOUN a play, film or television programme that is intended to make people laugh • *The film is a romantic comedy.*

float /fləʊt/ (floats, floating, floated) VERB to move slowly and gently through the air • *A yellow balloon floated past.*

flyboard /'flaɪˌbɔ:d/ (flyboards) NOUN ™ a machine that you put on your feet and that lets you fly over water using jets • *We had fun with a flyboard off the French coast.*

fuel /'fju:əl/ NOUN a substance such as coal or oil that is burned to provide heat or power • *They bought some fuel on the motorway.*

government /'gʌvənmənt/ (governments) NOUN the group of people who control and organise a country, a state or a city • *The government has decided to make changes.*

ingredient /ɪn'gri:diənt/ (ingredients) NOUN one of the things that you use to make something, especially when you are cooking • *Mix together all the ingredients.*

inventor /ɪn'ventə/ (inventors) NOUN a person who has thought of or made something, or

whose job is to think of or make things • *Who was the inventor of the telephone?*

laboratory /lə'bɒrətri/ (laboratories) NOUN a building or a room where scientific work is done • *He works in a research laboratory at the university.*

land /lænd/ (lands, landing, landed) VERB to arrive somewhere • *The plane landed just after 10 p.m.*

marathon /'mærəθən/ (marathons) NOUN a race in which people run a distance of 26 miles (= about 42 km) • *He is running in his first marathon next weekend.*

mash /mæʃ/ (mash, mashing, mashed) VERB to press food to make it soft • *Mash the bananas with a fork.*

pastry /'peɪstri/ NOUN a food made from flour, fat and water that is often used for making pies • *Roll out the pastry thinly.*

pick up /pɪk ʌp/ (picks up, picking up, picked up) PHRASAL VERB to collect someone or something from a place, often in a car • *Please could you pick me up at 5 p.m.?*

poke /pəʊk/ (pokes, poking, poked) VERB If something **pokes out from** another thing, you can see part of it behind or underneath the other thing. • *He saw the dog's nose poke out of the basket.*

seaweed /'si:wi:d/ NOUN a plant that grows in the sea • *We looked at the seaweed washed up on a beach.*

smell /smel/ (smells, smelling, smelled) VERB to have a quality that you notice by breathing in through your nose • *The soup smells delicious!*

sound /saʊnd/ (sounds, sounding, sounded) VERB used for describing your opinion of something • *It sounds like a wonderful idea to me.*

space /speɪs/ NOUN the area beyond the Earth's atmosphere, where the stars and planets are • *The six astronauts will spend ten days in space.*

traditional /trə'dɪʃənəl/ ADJECTIVE used when talking about a type of behaviour or a belief that has existed for a long time • *The band plays a lot of traditional Scottish music.*

training /'treɪnɪŋ/ NOUN preparation for a sports event • *He keeps fit through exercise and training.*

zero gravity /ˈzɪərəʊ ˌgrævɪti/ NOUN the state of having no weight, as in space • *There is room for the astronauts to float in zero gravity.*

TEST 6

at least /ət ˈliːst/ PHRASE not less than a particular number or amount • *Drink at least half a pint of milk each day.*

average /ˈævərɪdʒ/ ADJECTIVE ordinary • *He seemed to be a pleasant, average guy.*

bare /beə/ ADJECTIVE not covered by any clothing • *Jane's feet were bare.*

beat /biːt/ (beats) NOUN the rhythm of a piece of music • *Play some music with a steady beat.*

career /kəˈrɪə/ (careers) NOUN a job that you do for a long time, or the years of your life that you spend working • *She had a long career as a teacher.*

changing room /ˈtʃeɪndʒɪŋ ˌruːm/ (changing rooms) NOUN a room in a sports centre where you can change your clothes and usually have a shower • *I ran and hid in the changing room.*

charge /tʃɑːdʒ/ (charges, charging, charged) VERB to put electricity into a battery • *Alex forgot to charge his mobile phone.*

compare /kəmˈpeə/ (compares, comparing, compared) VERB to consider how things are different and how they are similar • *I use the Internet to compare prices.*

deaf /def/ ADJECTIVE unable to hear anything or unable to hear very well • *He is deaf in his left ear.*

delete /dɪˈliːt/ (deletes, deleting, deleted) VERB to remove something that has been stored on a computer • *He deleted files from the computer.*

delicious /dɪˈlɪʃəs/ ADJECTIVE very good to eat • *There was a wide choice of delicious meals.*

experience /ɪkˈspɪəriəns/ (experiences, experiencing, experienced) VERB If you experience something, you are affected by it. • *This is a way to experience music by your favourite bands.*

expert /ˈekspɜːt/ (experts) NOUN a person who knows a lot about a particular subject • *His brother is a computer expert.*

flow /fləʊ/ (flows, flowing, flowed) VERB to move somewhere in a steady and continuous way • *A stream flowed gently down into the valley.*

graduate /ˈgrædʒuət/ (graduates, graduating, graduated) VERB to complete your studies at college or university • *Her son has just graduated from Oxford.*

harmonica /hɑːˈmɒnɪkə/ (harmonicas) NOUN a small musical instrument which you play by moving it across your lips and blowing • *The national anthem was performed on the harmonica.*

hearing /ˈhɪərɪŋ/ NOUN the sense that makes it possible for you to be aware of sounds • *His hearing was excellent.*

light up /laɪt ʌp/ (lights up, lighting up, lit up) PHRASAL VERB If something lights up, it becomes bright, usually by shining light on it • *The fireworks will light up the sky.*

location setting /ləʊˈkeɪʃən ˌsetɪŋ/ (locations settings) NOUN The location setting on a mobile phone is a way of showing where you are so that you can get information about that area. • *Remember to turn off your location setting.*

locker /ˈlɒkə/ (lockers) NOUN a small cupboard with a lock, that you keep things in at a school or at a sports club • *You can rent a locker for the day.*

log in/into /lɒg ɪn/ɪntuː/ (logs in/into, logging in/into, logged in/into) PHRASAL VERB If you log into a computer, or if you log in, you type a special secret word so that you can start using a computer or a website. • *She turned on her computer and logged in.*

melt /melt/ (melts, melting, melted) VERB When a solid substance melts away, it changes to a liquid because of heat • *The snow melted away.*

northeast /ˌnɔːˈθiːst/ NOUN the direction that is between north and east • *They live in Jerusalem, more than 250 miles to the north-east.*

perform /pəˈfɔːm/ (performs, performing, performed) VERB to do a play, a piece of music or a dance in front of an audience • *They will be performing works by Bach.*

rafting (raftings) NOUN the sport of travelling down a river on a raft • *I enjoy water sports such as boating, fishing and rafting.*

rainbow /ˈreɪnbəʊ/ (rainbows) NOUN A rainbow of colours is a wide range of bright colours. • *On the sofa was a rainbow of coloured cushions.*

rare /reə/ ADJECTIVE not seen or heard very often • *This is one of the rarest birds in the world.*

rhythm /ˈrɪðəm/ **(rhythms)** NOUN a regular pattern of sounds or movements • *Listen to the rhythms of jazz.*

sign up /saɪn ʌp/ **(signs up, signing up, signed up)** PHRASAL VERB If you **sign up** for an activity, you agree to do it. • *She signed up for dance classes.*

skyscraper /ˈskaɪskreɪpə/ **(skyscrapers)** NOUN a very tall building in a city • *This building is the country's tallest skyscraper.*

slide /slaɪd/ **(slides)** NOUN a smooth slope which people go down for fun • *We made icy slides in the playground.*

solo /ˈsəʊləʊ/ ADVERB done by one person • *Lindbergh flew solo across the Atlantic.*

species /ˈspiːʃiz/ **(species)** NOUN a related group of plants or animals • *Many species could disappear from our Earth.*

unexpected /ˌʌnɪkˈspektɪd/ ADJECTIVE surprising, because you do not think it will happen • *Scientists have made an unexpected discovery.*

wildlife /ˈwaɪldlaɪf/ **(wildlife)** NOUN used for talking about the animals and other living things that live in nature • *The area is rich in wildlife.*

TEST 7

ability /əˈbɪlɪti/ **(abilities)** NOUN a quality or a skill that makes it possible for you to do something • *Her drama teacher noticed her acting ability.*

calligraphy /kəˈlɪgrəfi/ NOUN beautiful handwriting which uses a brush or a special pen • *The invitations were written in fancy calligraphy.*

canoeing /kəˈnuːɪŋ/ NOUN the sport of using and racing a canoe • *They went canoeing in the wilds of Canada.*

confident /ˈkɒnfɪdənt/ ADJECTIVE feeling sure about your own abilities and ideas • *In time he became more confident and relaxed.*

culture /ˈkʌltʃə/ **(cultures)** NOUN the way of life, the traditions and beliefs of a particular group of people • *I live in the city among people from different cultures.*

electronic gadget /ɪlekˈtrɒnɪk gædʒɪt/ **(electronic gadgets)** NOUN a small machine or useful object which uses electricity • *The shop sells computers and other electronic gadgets.*

ground /graʊnd/ NOUN the surface of the Earth or the floor of a room • *He fell to the ground.*

lifelike /ˈlaɪflaɪk/ ADJECTIVE A **lifelike** work of art looks very like the person or thing that it is supposed to be. • *The picture was so lifelike, you wanted to eat it.*

mask /mɑːsk/ **(masks)** NOUN something that you wear over your face to protect it or to hide it • *Wear a mask to protect yourself from the smoke.*

mental health /ˈmentəl ˌhelθ/ NOUN the condition of a person's mind • *People now feel happy to talk about mental health.*

national park /ˈnæʃənəl ˌpɑːk/ **(national parks)** NOUN a large area of land protected by the government because of its natural beauty, plants or animals • *There are 16 national parks in Alaska.*

process /ˈprəʊses/ **(processes, processing, processed)** VERB to deal with • *It is all to do with how our brains process information.*

rock climbing /ˈrɒk ˌklaɪmɪŋ/ NOUN the activity of climbing rocks or mountains • *The kids can enjoy activities like rock climbing , mountain biking and swimming.*

statue /ˈstætʃuː/ **(statues)** NOUN a large model of a person or an animal, made of stone or metal • *She gave me a stone statue of a horse.*

stick to /stɪk/ **(sticks, sticking, stuck)** PHRASAL VERB to stick to something is to keep doing it • *We are waiting to see if he sticks to his promise.*

survivor /səˈvaɪvə/ **(survivors)** NOUN someone who gets through a difficult or dangerous time • *Bob has shown time and time again that he is a true survivor.*

unfortunately /ʌnˈfɔːtʃʊnətli/ ADVERB used for showing that you are sorry about something • *Unfortunately, I don't have time to stay.*

wax /wæks/ **(waxes)** NOUN a solid, slightly shiny substance that is used for making candles • *The candle wax melted in the heat.*

wild /waɪld/ NOUN Animals that live in the wild live freely and are not looked after by people. • *Fewer than a thousand giant pandas still live in the wild.*

---

come across /kʌm əˈkrɒs/ **(comes across, coming across, came across)** PHRASAL VERB to find something or someone, or meet them by chance • *I came across a photo of my grandparents when I was looking for my diary.*

cure /kjʊə/ **(cures)** NOUN something that makes someone become well again • *There is still no cure for a cold.*

deal with /diːl wɪð/ **(deals with, dealing with, dealt with)** PHRASAL VERB to give your attention to someone or something • *She often has to deal with complaints from customers.*

diet /ˈdaɪət/ **(diets)** NOUN the type of food that you regularly eat • *It's never too late to improve your diet.*

discover /dɪsˈkʌvə/ **(discovers, discovering, discovered)** VERB to be the first person to find or use a new place, substance or method • *Who was the first European to discover America?*

fall behind /fɔːl bɪˈhaɪnd/ **(falls behind, falling behind, fell behind)** PHRASAL VERB to fail to make progress or move forward as fast as other people • *Some of the students fell behind in their work.*

gallery /ˈɡæləri/ **(galleries)** NOUN a place where people go to look at art • *We visited an art gallery.*

lecture /ˈlektʃə/ **(lectures)** NOUN a talk that someone gives in order to teach people about a particular subject • *We attended a lecture by Professor Eric Robinson.*

miracle /ˈmɪrəkəl/ **(miracles)** NOUN a surprising and lucky event that you cannot explain • *It's a miracle that Chris survived the accident.*

overweight /ˌəʊvəˈweɪt/ ADJECTIVE weighing more than is considered healthy or attractive • *Since I started running, I'm no longer overweight.*

portion /ˈpɔːʃən/ **(portions)** NOUN the amount of food that is given to one person at a meal • *The portions were huge.*

regularly /ˈreɡjʊlə/ ADVERB happening often • *He writes regularly for the magazine.*

relate /rɪˈleɪt/ **(relates, relating, related)** VERB to be about a particular subject • *We are collecting all the information relating to the crime.*

species /ˈspiːʃiz/ NOUN a related group of plants or animals • *Many species could disappear from our Earth.*

stressed /strest/ ADJECTIVE feeling very worried because of difficulties in your life • *What situations make you feel stressed?*

suit /suːt/ **(suits, suiting, suited)** VERB to make you look attractive • *Green suits you.*

supplies /səˈplaɪz/ PLURAL NOUN food, equipment and other important things that are provided for people • *What happens when there are no more food supplies?*

Audio scripts

These are the audio scripts for the Listening and Speaking parts of the tests. Listen to the audio online at: www.collins.co.uk/eltresources

TEST 1   LISTENING

Part 1

Track 01

Key English Test for Schools, Listening.
There are five parts to the test. You will hear each piece twice.
We will now stop for a moment.
Please ask any questions now, because you must not speak during the test.
Now look at the instructions for Part 1.
For each question, choose the correct answer.
Look at Question 1.

1 *Which is the most popular place?*

Woman: Look! The beach is full of people. What are we going to do?
Man: Maybe we could go to the café first and go to the beach later, when some of them leave.
Woman: I suppose so, but I think it'll rain this afternoon.
Man: How about the swimming pool? We haven't been there for ages!

Now listen again.

2 *What does John like to do on the bus to school?*

Woman: Do you often read on the bus to school, John?
John: No, I don't really like it. I sometimes look at magazines, but reading makes me feel sick.
Woman: Me too! So what do you do?
John: I just listen to music. You?
Woman: Oh, I just chat and text people.

Now listen again.

3 *When does the girl have a geography lesson?*

Marcus: Hey, Gloria, what's your next lesson?
Gloria: English, and I've got geography after that.
Marcus: But today's Wednesday. I thought you had geography on Friday.
Gloria: I do, but I also have geography today. Listen, Marcus, when do you have chemistry?
Marcus: On Tuesdays and Thursdays.
Gloria: Great! I've also got chemistry on Thursday. Can you help me with my homework in the afternoon?

Now listen again.

4 *When does badminton practice usually start?*

Boy: When does badminton practice usually start? Is it four fifteen?

Girl: No, at four o'clock.
Boy: So why did it start later last week?
Girl: Because some students were doing an exam in the gym. It may start later, at four thirty next time because there's an exam next week as well.

Now listen again.

5 *What present will they buy?*

Girl: What shall we buy Max for his birthday?
Boy: We could buy him football socks or maybe a football shirt. He's a big sports fan.
Girl: Socks?! That's boring! How about something like a sports bag for his kit or a ticket to a big match?
Boy: He bought a bag last week and he's already a member of the football club. How about a cap of his favourite team?
Girl: Yes, he'll love that.

Now listen again.
That is the end of Part 1.

Part 2

Track 02

Now look at Part 2.
For each question, write the correct answer in the gap. Write one word or a number or a date or a time. Look at questions 6–10 now.
You have ten seconds.
You will hear a woman talking to some people about a new library.

Woman: Hello, everyone, and welcome to this talk about the great new library in our city. It opens on 5th June, this Saturday, in fact. It's a beautiful modern building surrounded by a large garden, and it's a wonderful place to spend time and explore.
It will be open to the public seven days a week and the opening hours will be from 8 a.m. until 8 p.m. every day. However, on Friday evenings in the summer, there will also be an outdoor cinema in the garden, so closing time on that day will be four hours later, at midnight.
It's very easy to get to the library. The number 195 bus from the town centre takes just 20 minutes, and the bus stop is opposite the entrance to the library. You can also come by underground. Underground tickets from the city centre cost £3.50 and bus tickets are £2.00.

To find out about underground and bus times, please call our main office on 020 876 9719. That's 020 876 9719. Now, let me tell you a little about ...

Now listen again.
That is the end of Part 2.

Part 3

Track 03

Now look at Part 3.
For each question, choose the correct answer. Look at questions 11–15 now. You have twenty seconds.
You will hear Tom talking to his dad about his birthday party.

Tom:	Dad, can I invite all my friends to my party?
Dad:	Hmm ... I don't know, Tom.
Tom:	Please, Dad! It's my 13th birthday. It's special this year!
Dad:	More special than last year?
Tom:	Yes! I stop being a child and become a teenager!
Dad:	OK, OK. How many friends?
Tom:	Twenty-five!
Dad:	What?! There were only fourteen last year!
Tom:	Oh, come on, Dad! In Brazil and the USA, they have really big parties when they are thirteen. My friend Eva, her mum's American, and Eva had a huge party. And thirteenth birthday parties are very popular in the UK now.
Dad:	So what was the party like?
Tom:	It was in a disco! Eva's mum ordered food from a restaurant, and we danced. And there were lots of people, so they couldn't have the party at her house. Her friends came, and her grandparents, aunts, uncles. Dad, do we have to invite our relatives?
Dad:	Not all of them.
Tom:	Cool! I'll invite the kids next door!
Dad:	No, Tom! We can't invite everyone. Our house is too small!

Now listen again.
That is the end of Part 3.

Part 4

Track 04

Now look at Part 4.
For each question, choose the correct answer.

16 *You will hear a customer talking to a shop assistant. Why does he want to return the jacket?*

Man:	I'd like to return this jacket, please.
Woman:	Yes, sure. Can you tell me why? Is it too small?
Man:	The size and the colour are fine, but there's a hole in it. I didn't see it until I got home.
Woman:	OK. That's no problem.

Now listen again.

17 *You will hear a girl talking about her best friend, Danielle. What does Danielle look like?*

Girl:	My best friend is Danielle. We met in primary school. We walk to school together every morning. Danielle and I look very different. She's got short, straight, fair hair and I've got long, straight, dark hair. Her eyes are green and mine are blue. But we both love doing the same things and we have a lot of fun together.

Now listen again.

18 *You will hear a girl talking to her dentist. Why is she unhappy?*

Dentist:	What happened, Kim?
Kim:	I had an accident while I was skateboarding. I fell and hit my mouth. There was a lot of blood!
Dentist:	Oh, how terrible! Are you in pain?
Kim:	It hurt a lot at first, but not now. I just have half a tooth now!
Dentist:	Don't worry. Let's see what we can do.

Now listen again.

19 *You will hear two friends talking about their plans. What do they decide to do at the weekend?*

Man:	Would you like to go shopping this weekend?
Woman:	Hmm ... I don't need to buy anything.
Man:	How about watching the match on TV?
Woman:	I don't want to sit on a sofa all afternoon.
Man:	We could go to the stadium...
Woman:	I don't want to watch our team losing again. They're terrible!
Man:	I'd rather do something active. Let's go to the beach.
Woman:	OK.

Now listen again.

20 *You will hear a a mother talking to her son, Harry. What does Harry's mum ask him to do?*

Mum:	Harry, your room is a mess!
Harry:	Not anymore, Mum! I've put everything away.
Mum:	Good, but have you done the other things I asked you to do?
Harry:	Not yet. You said you were going to fix my skateboard this morning.
Mum:	Well, empty the kitchen bin first and we'll fix it afterwards. And then I must take the dog for a walk.

Now listen again.
That is the end of Part 4.

Part 5

Track 05

Now look at Part 5.
For each question, choose the correct answer.
Look at Questions 21 to 25 now.
You have 15 seconds.
You will hear Billy talking to Lucy about a camping trip.
What will each person bring to the camp?

Billy:	Is everything ready for the camping trip, Lucy?
Lucy:	Yes, nearly, Billy. I've made lots of sandwiches for the car journey. The others are bringing the camping equipment.
Billy:	What are they bringing?
Lucy:	We can't light fires at the camp, so Mark is bringing something to cook on.
Billy:	Good idea! And I can bring some cups and plates from home. I've got some paper ones left from my party.
Lucy:	Thanks, Billy, but don't worry about the plates. We've got lots from last time. Alicia also wanted to bring plates, but I told her the same thing I'm telling you. So I said she should just bring her new tent for the girls.
Billy:	Oh yes! Andrew told me about it. It's great! He saw it at Alicia's house. Six people can sleep in it.
Lucy:	Tina's coming too. She and her family go camping a lot, so she's bringing five sleeping bags and two folding chairs.
Billy:	I hope Emma can bring her camping lamp. The torch we used last time didn't give off much light.
Lucy:	Yes, she said she would.

Now listen again.
That is the end of Part 5. You now have six minutes to write your answers on the answer sheet.
That is the end of the test.

TEST 1   SPEAKING

Part 1

Track 06

Examiner:	Good morning. Can I have your mark sheets, please? I'm Hannah Jones. And this is Keith Mantell. What's your name, Candidate A?
Candidate A:	My name's Alicia Perez.
Examiner:	And what's your name, Candidate B?
[PAUSE FOR YOU TO ANSWER]	
Examiner:	Candidate B, how old are you?
[PAUSE FOR YOU TO ANSWER]	

Examiner:	Where do you come from, Candidate B?
[PAUSE FOR YOU TO ANSWER]	
Examiner:	Thank you. Candidate A, how old are you?
Candidate A:	I'm thirteen.
Examiner:	Where do you come from?
Candidate A:	I come from Valencia in Spain.
Examiner:	Thank you.
Examiner:	Now, let's talk about sport. Candidate A, what sports do you like?
Candidate A:	I like playing hockey very much. I also enjoy tennis, but I don't play it. I just watch it on TV.
Examiner:	How often do you do sport?
Candidate A:	I play hockey twice a week after school and I have a PE lesson three times a week.
Examiner:	Candidate B, what kind of sports do you do?
[PAUSE FOR YOU TO ANSWER]	
Examiner:	Where do you do sports, Candidate B?
[PAUSE FOR YOU TO ANSWER]	
Examiner:	Now Candidate A, please tell me something about a sport that you don't like.
Candidate A:	I don't really like sports like skateboarding because they're too dangerous. And I don't like golf. I think it's boring.
Examiner:	Now, let's talk about clothes. Candidate B, what kind of clothes do you usually wear?
[PAUSE FOR YOU TO ANSWER]	
Examiner:	How often do you buy new clothes, Candidate B?
[PAUSE FOR YOU TO ANSWER]	
Examiner:	Candidate A, where do you like shopping for clothes?
Candidate A:	I go to the big department stores in the city centre because I can find anything I want there.
Examiner:	What are your favourite clothes?
Candidate A:	I like following fashions and I wear clothes that I see in magazines.
Examiner:	Now Candidate B, please tell me something about the kind of clothes you don't like to wear.
[PAUSE FOR YOU TO ANSWER]	
Examiner:	Thank you.

Part 2

Track 07

Examiner:	Now, in this part of the test you are going to talk together. Here are some pictures that show different free-time activities.

Do you like these different free-time activities? Say why or why not. I'll say that again.

Do you like these different free-time activities? Say why or why not.

All right? Now, talk together.

Candidate A: I don't like most of these free-time activities because I prefer to do activities indoors. I enjoy taking photos, but I don't use a camera. I always use my phone. How about you?

[PAUSE FOR YOU TO ANSWER]

Candidate A: Which activity do you like the best?

[PAUSE FOR YOU TO ANSWER]

Candidate A: I like dancing and listening to music.

Examiner: Candidate A, do you think going camping is fun?

Candidate A: No, I don't, because I don't like sleeping outside. It's too noisy and uncomfortable.

Examiner: Candidate B, do you think going surfing with friends is dangerous?

[PAUSE FOR YOU TO ANSWER]

Examiner: So, Candidate A, which of these free-time activities do you like best?

Candidate A: I like going to museums and learning about people from the past.

Examiner: And you, Candidate B, which of these free-time activities do you like doing with your friends?

[PAUSE FOR YOU TO ANSWER]

Examiner: Thank you.
Now, do you prefer doing free-time activities after school or at the weekend, Candidate B?

[PAUSE FOR YOU TO ANSWER]

Examiner: Why is that, Candidate B?

[PAUSE FOR YOU TO ANSWER]

Examiner: And what about you, Candidate A? Do you prefer doing free-time activities after school or at the weekend?

Candidate A: I prefer doing activities after school.

Examiner: Do you prefer being active or relaxing at home, Candidate A?

Candidate A: I prefer relaxing at home because I can read my favourite books.

Examiner: And you, Candidate B? Do you prefer being active or relaxing at home?

[PAUSE FOR YOU TO ANSWER]

Examiner: Why, Candidate B?

[PAUSE FOR YOU TO ANSWER]

Examiner: Thank you. That is the end of the test.

TEST 2   LISTENING

Part 1

Track 08

Key English Test for Schools, Listening
There are five parts to the test. You will hear each piece twice.
We will now stop for a moment.
Please ask any questions now, because you must not speak during the test.
Now look at the instructions for Part 1.
For each question, choose the correct answer.
Look at Question 1.

1 *Who is the girl's brother?*

Boy: I've never met your brother. Does he look like you?

Girl: Yes, but he's blond, not dark, and when he was younger, his hair was long. Now it's short, like mine.

Boy: Is he tall like you?

Girl: No, but he's five years younger than me! He says he wants to be tall when he grows up so he can be a professional basketball player.

Now listen again.

2 *What project did Kim finish for school?*

Man: How's school, Kim?

Kim: Not bad. I had a maths exam this week. It was quite hard.

Man: Have you finished your history project yet?

Kim: No, I was working on my geography project this week. I gave it to the teacher on Wednesday. Now I'm doing my history one. Did you know: there were more than 40 kings of France?!

Now listen again.

3 *What will Mark have for lunch?*

Woman: Mark, let's get something to eat at the new café in town.

Mark: OK. I hope they have nice salads.

Woman: You're very good. You eat a lot of healthy food. I eat too many burgers.

Mark: Why don't you have an omelette? Or you could have mushroom soup. You love mushrooms!

Now listen again.

4 *What time does Sam's hockey lesson start?*

Sam: Dad, can you pick me up after school at two thirty? I have hockey practice at the sports centre at three.

Dad:	I'm not sure, Sam, My dentist's appointment is at two. Can you walk there?
Sam:	No, I don't want to be late. The coach gets angry if we aren't there on time.
Dad:	OK. I'll try to change my appointment to half past three.

Now listen again.

5 *Which building is nearest to them?*

Man:	Excuse me, could you show me where the library is on this map?
Woman:	Yes. It's on Field Street. We're here, look, next to the cinema. Just go straight and take the first left. Continue past the supermarket and it's the second building on your right.
Man:	How long does it take?
Woman:	Hmm ... about ten minutes.
Man:	Thanks!

Now listen again.
That is the end of Part 1.

Part 2

Track 09

Now look at Part 2.
For each question, write the correct answer in the gap. Write one word or a number or a date or a time. Look at questions 6–10 now.
You have ten seconds.
You will hear a boy telling people about his business.

| Henry: | Hi! My name's Henry Divani and I want to tell you a little about my business. People are surprised when I tell them I have a business because I'm only fourteen. It started when I was ten years old, after I wrote a book for children called The Adventures of Ernest, that's E-R-N-E-S-T. I published the book on the Internet with my mum's help. At first, we sold the book for £9.99, but not many people bought it. Then, we changed the price to £1.99 and we sold ten thousand copies of the book in the first month, and fifty thousand in the second. It was amazing! So I set up a website and started selling things like bags and T-shirts with characters from my book on them. Now I'm writing my second book. I wake up at half past five every morning and write for two hours before school. Then, after school I write for another two hours. It's a lot of work, but I love sharing my stories! |

Now listen again.
That is the end of Part 2.

Part 3

Track 10

Now look at Part 3.
For each question, choose the correct answer. Look at questions 11–15 now. You have 20 seconds.
You will hear Lily talking to her friend, Ethan, about an accident.

Lily:	Hi, Ethan. I heard you had an accident. How are you? What did you break? Your arm?
Ethan:	No, my foot. I slipped on some ice. I also cut my hands when I fell.
Lily:	You were lucky not to hurt your head! Did you call an ambulance?
Ethan:	I didn't have my phone with me, so I shouted for help. My neighbour heard me, he called my dad, and Dad drove me to the hospital.
Lily:	What happens now?
Ethan:	I have to stay home for a few days. The doctor says I'll be OK in four weeks, so I can play in the match next month!
Lily:	And don't forget, you have to study for the test on Wednesday.
Ethan:	But I won't be at school on Wednesday.
Lily:	Don't worry, Mr Smith will make you do it later!
Ethan:	That's awful! No football tomorrow and now no video games and no TV – because of a stupid test!
Lily:	Well, I'll help you with the lessons you miss and I'll bring you your homework. And if you're nice to me, I'll visit you every day after school!

Now listen again.
That is the end of Part 3.

Part 4

Track 11

Now look at Part 4.
For each question, choose the correct answer.

16 *You will hear two friends talking about the best way to go home. Which is the shortest way?*

Woman:	What about going home across the fields? We'll be there in an hour.
Man:	An hour? I'm not sure. It looks like rain.
Woman:	Then let's go over the hill. It will only take us about 45 minutes. Or we can go around the lake.
Man:	That will take us one and a half hours.
Woman:	Yes, you're right.

Now listen again.

17 *You will hear Ivan talking to his friend Megan. What did Megan do about her problem?*

| Ivan: | How's your backache, Megan? |

Megan:	It's better. I was very bad after the race, so Mum took me to the doctor.
Ivan:	Did she give you any exercises to do?
Megan:	No, she told me to try swimming. It helped a lot! I'm also going to buy some special shoes for long distance running.
Ivan:	Good idea!

Now listen again.

18 *You will hear a girl talking to a shop assistant. What can't she do?*

Girl:	Can I try on these skirts, please?
Assistant:	Yes, of course. How many have you got?
Girl:	Er ... six.
Assistant:	I'm afraid you can only take five items into the changing rooms at a time.
Girl:	OK. Can I leave this one with you?
Assistant:	Yes, and I'll put it over here and you can try it on later.

Now listen again.

19 *You will hear a boy talking to his mother. What does she want him to do?*

Boy:	Mum, do you know where my football kit is?
Mum:	I washed it and put it in your wardrobe.
Boy:	Thanks, Mum!
Mum:	You need to clean your football boots more often and not leave them in your bag. They weren't cheap. I won't buy you any more if you don't look after them.

Now listen again.

20 *You will hear a teacher talking to a student. Why is he talking to her?*

Mr Jones:	Well done, Maria. Your project was very interesting. You found a lot of great information about the subject.
Maria:	Thank you, Mr Jones.
Mr Jones:	I'd like to put your project on the school website. I think everyone will be interested to learn about our town. Is that all right?
Maria:	Yes, of course. That's great!

Now listen again.
That is the end of Part 4.

Part 5

Track 12

Now look at Part 5.
For each question, choose the correct answer.
Look at Questions 21 to 25 now.
You have 15 seconds.
You will hear Tom and Ivy planning what they would like to do in the school holidays. What activity will they do on each day?

Tom:	It's Sunday already, and we've only got one week of holiday, so let's plan.
Ivy:	Well, we can go on a boat trip tomorrow.

Tom:	OK, and let's ask Mum if we can go and see the animals on Tuesday. I'd love to see the baby elephants.
Ivy:	Good idea. But I want to go swimming too.
Tom:	Mum said we should do that on our last day.
Ivy:	Oh, all right. Now, what about looking around the old town on Wednesday? We can join a group and someone will show us around and tell us about the history of the place.
Tom:	Yeah, OK. And I want to go shopping.
Ivy:	I don't think we'll have time on Wednesday.
Tom:	OK. Well, on Thursday, we could visit the castle, or the museum, or go to the market.
Ivy:	We can't do everything, but I'd like to look at the fruit and vegetables for sale. Some of the fruit is really strange.
Tom:	Yeah, that would be fun.
Ivy:	And then on Friday we can buy gifts for everybody. I saw some fantastic jewellery and other stuff.
Tom:	And we can go swimming on Saturday.
Ivy:	Great!

Now listen again.
That is the end of Part 5. You now have six minutes to write your answers on the answer sheet.
That is the end of the test.

TEST 2   SPEAKING

Part 1

Track 13

Examiner:	Good afternoon.
	Can I have your mark sheets, please?
	I'm David Dolan. And this is Anne Marshall.
	What's your name, Candidate A?
Candidate A:	My name's Gabriel Charpentier.
Examiner:	And what's your name, Candidate B?
[PAUSE FOR YOU TO ANSWER]	
Examiner:	Candidate B, how old are you?
[PAUSE FOR YOU TO ANSWER]	
Examiner:	And where do you live, Candidate B?
[PAUSE FOR YOU TO ANSWER]	
Examiner:	Thank you.
	Candidate A, how old are you?
Candidate A:	I'm thirteen.
Examiner:	Where do you live?
Candidate A:	I live in Lyon.
Examiner:	Thank you.
Examiner:	Now, let's talk about homework.

	Candidate A, how often do you get homework each week?
Candidate A:	I usually get homework two or three times a week, and always on a Friday so we can study during the weekend.
Examiner:	For which subject do you do the most homework?
Candidate A:	I usually do the most homework for maths and French because we have some important exams soon.
Examiner:	Candidate B, why do you think young people usually dislike homework?

[PAUSE FOR YOU TO ANSWER]

| Examiner: | Do you think it's important to do your homework, Candidate B? |

[PAUSE FOR YOU TO ANSWER]

Examiner:	Now Candidate A, please tell me something about a homework project you enjoyed.
Candidate A:	I enjoyed a science project I did last month. We had to make a model of a space rocket. It was fun!
Examiner:	Now, let's talk about food. Candidate B, what do you usually have for breakfast?

[PAUSE FOR YOU TO ANSWER]

| Examiner: | What food do you eat at school, Candidate B? |

[PAUSE FOR YOU TO ANSWER]

Examiner:	Candidate A, what sweet food do you like to eat?
Candidate A:	I'm not keen on sweet food, but if it's someone's birthday, I eat some cake. I sometimes eat chocolate at the weekend.
Examiner:	What's your favourite food?
Candidate A:	My favourite food is fresh vegetables and fruit. I eat a lot of salads. I also like simple food like omelettes or soup.
Examiner:	Now Candidate B, please tell me something about the kind of food you don't like to eat.

[PAUSE FOR YOU TO ANSWER]

Part 2

Track 14

| Examiner: | Now, in this part of the test you are going to talk together. Here are some pictures that show different types of holiday. Do you like these different types of holiday? Say why or why not. I'll say that again. Do you like these different types of holiday? Say why or why not. |

| | All right? Now, talk together. |
| Candidate A: | I think it's fun to go camping and I enjoy adventure holidays. How about you? |

[PAUSE FOR YOU TO ANSWER]

| Candidate A | Why do you like beach holidays? |

[PAUSE FOR YOU TO ANSWER]

| Candidate A: | Well, I don't like holidays where you sit all day and do nothing. I like to be active on holiday and there are lots of interesting activities to do on adventure holidays. You can climb mountains, do bungee jumping, go rafting ... |

[PAUSE FOR YOU TO ANSWER]

Examiner:	Candidate A, why do you enjoy camping?
Candidate A:	Because I love sleeping in a tent and cooking food over a fire. We're active during the day and at night we tell stories and sing songs. It's fun.
Examiner:	Candidate B, why do you enjoy city breaks?

[PAUSE FOR YOU TO ANSWER]

Examiner:	So Candidate A, which of these holidays do you like the best?
Candidate A:	If I have to choose between a camping holiday and an adventure holiday, I'll choose a camping holiday because I enjoy nature and exploring the countryside.
Examiner:	And you, Candidate B, which of these holidays do you like the best?

[PAUSE FOR YOU TO ANSWER]

| Examiner: | Thank you. Now, would you prefer to go on holiday with your family or friends, Candidate B? |

[PAUSE FOR YOU TO ANSWER]

| Examiner: | Why, Candidate B? |

[PAUSE FOR YOU TO ANSWER]

Examiner:	And what about you, Candidate A? Would you prefer to go on holiday with your family or friends?
Candidate A:	I'd prefer to go on holiday with my family.
Examiner:	Why?
Candidate A:	Well, I've got two older brothers and they're at university, so I don't see them often. When they come on holiday with me and my parents, we have a lot of fun together.
Examiner:	Do you prefer holidays in your country or holidays in other countries, Candidate A?

Candidate A: I've never been to another country! But I think I prefer holidays in my country. There are lots of great places to see, and I haven't seen them all.

Examiner: And you, Candidate B? Do you prefer holidays in your country or holidays in other countries?

[PAUSE FOR YOU TO ANSWER]

Examiner: Thank you. That is the end of the test.

TEST 3   LISTENING

Part 1

Track 15

Key English Test for Schools, Listening.
There are five parts to the test. You will hear each piece twice.
We will now stop for a moment.
Please ask any questions now, because you must not speak during the test.
Now look at the instructions for Part 1.
For each question, choose the correct answer.
Look at Question 1.

1   *Where do they think the boy left his phone?*

Boy: Oh no! I can't find my phone!

Girl: Did you leave it in the classroom after the maths lesson?

Boy: No, I took it with me. We had lunch after that and I checked my messages in the canteen.

Girl: Maybe you left it in the computer room while we were working on our project.

Boy: Good idea! I'll go and look there now.

Now listen again.

2   *How did the family celebrate Lisa's grandmother's birthday?*

Boy: How was your weekend, Lisa?

Lisa: It was great! It was Granny's birthday.

Boy: How did you celebrate?

Lisa: Mum wanted to take her to a restaurant, but Dad thought she'd enjoy going to see a tennis match – she loves tennis! But the tickets were sold out. So we had a barbecue in the garden. It was more fun than going to a restaurant.

Now listen again.

3   *Who got the cat off the roof?*

Boy: So, what happened to your cat Bubbles?

Girl: He couldn't get off the roof of the house.

Boy: How did you get him down?

Girl: I wanted to call the fire brigade, but Mum got a ladder from our neighbour, Mr Jones. She climbed up to the roof

and Bubbles ran to her. We think he climbed onto the roof from a tree.

Boy: What a story!

Now listen again.

4   *Which photo won the competition?*

Woman: Well done for winning the photo competition!

Boy: Thank you! I took the photo when we went to the lake last month.

Woman: Was that the one you showed me of the rabbits in the forest?

Boy: No, it was the close-up photo of the bee on a flower.

Woman: That was a beautiful photo!

Now listen again.

5   *What time does the film start?*

Boy: What time does the film start? Seven forty-five?

Girl: No, it begins at eight fifteen.

Boy: Are you sure? I thought it was earlier. The bus is every fifteen minutes, so if you're right about the time, we should leave at seven. I want to have time to buy popcorn before the film!

Girl: I'm right. I checked online, so we need to leave soon.

Now listen again.
That is the end of Part 1.

Part 2

Track 16

Now look at Part 2.
For each question, write the correct answer in the gap.
Write one word or a number or a date or a time. Look at questions 6–10 now.
You have ten seconds.
You will hear a teacher talking to a group of students about a camping trip.

Woman: Hello, everyone. I've got some important information about the camping trip on Saturday, so listen carefully. The coach leaves at seven thirty in the morning. We're meeting in front of the Pankhurst building – that's P-A-N-K-H-U-R-S-T. We can only wait ten minutes if you're late, so please be on time! We'll be away for three days, from Saturday morning until Monday evening. We get back at about 10 p.m. The journey to the campsite takes three hours. The coach will stop after an hour and a half at a service station. You'll have time to go to the bathroom and buy a snack. We won't have lunch until we reach the campsite and we've put up our tents. Also, it's going to be sunny, so make sure you wear a hat, bring a bottle of water, wear trainers or comfortable shoes and don't forget sun cream. OK, any questions?

Now listen again.
That is the end of Part 2.

Part 3

Track 17

Now look at Part 3.
For each question, choose the correct answer. Look at questions 11–15 now. You have twenty seconds.
You will hear Oscar talking to his friend Emily about going to a concert.

Oscar:	Hi Emily, are you free on Saturday? Tom and I are going to a rock concert. Would you like to come?
Emily:	Thanks, Oscar, but I'm not into rock music.
Oscar:	This band is different. They mix rock and pop, and they even play classical guitars and violins. Come on! It'll be fun!
Emily:	OK! I'll come! Shall we meet at the concert hall? I can get the train or the bus.
Oscar:	No, don't do that. Mum said she'll drive us.
Emily:	What about Tom?
Oscar:	Oh, he lives near the concert hall, so he'll take the train or bus – or walk. I hope he isn't late. They're only selling tickets at the entrance. We have to get there early because hundreds of people want to see the band.
Emily:	Sounds good.
Oscar:	And afterwards, we can go to that new pizza restaurant in the shopping centre in town. Tom's already been there because it's near his house. He says it's really good.
Emily:	Great! I love pizza.

Now listen again.
That is the end of Part 3.

Part 4

Track 18

Now look at Part 4.
For each question, choose the correct answer.

16 *You will hear a man talking about feeling ill. What did he do?*

Man:	I've had a high temperature for three days so I went to the doctor this morning. He said I have the flu and I need to get some rest. He didn't give me any medicine. He said the best thing I can do to get better is stay in bed, keep warm and drink lots of water.

Now listen again.

17 *You will hear a boy talking to his friend Sue. What did Sue forget to buy?*

Boy:	Do we have everything we need, Sue?
Sue:	I think so. I bought burgers and sausages. We can grill them on the barbecue. I also got snacks, lemonade and lots of ice cream!
Boy:	We need to make some salads, too. Lisa doesn't eat meat.
Sue:	I forgot about that. I'll have to go to the shop again.

Now listen again.

18 *You will hear two friends talking about a club. Why is Joseph talking to Katie?*

Joseph:	Hi Katie. You're a member of the rugby cub. Can you tell me about it?
Katie:	Sure, Joseph. What do you want to know?
Joseph:	Well, is it for beginners? I want to try it during the summer holidays when I have some free time.
Katie:	Yes, it's for everyone and the coach is great. You'll really like it.

Now listen again.

19 *You will hear two friends talking. Where are they?*

Girl:	OK, the books are on the second floor. We can take the lift.
Boy:	We can go there first and you can look for something about famous artists. Then I want to look at the jeans. And then we'll go to the café for lunch. I'm hungry.
Girl:	OK. And we must go to the post office so I can post my letter.

Now listen again.

20 *You will hear two friends talking. Where will they go first?*

Girl:	What time does your cousin's plane arrive?
Boy:	At three forty-five, so we must be at the airport by half past three.
Girl:	OK. Shall we go by bus?
Boy:	No, it takes too long. Let's take the bus from the stop near my house to the underground and then take the train. The station is next to the airport. It takes 20 minutes.

Now listen again.
That is the end of Part 4.

Part 5

Track 19

Now look at Part 5.
For each question, choose the correct answer.
Look at Questions 21 to 25 now.
You have 15 seconds.

You will hear Matt talking to a friend about hobbies.
Which hobby does each person do?

Girl:	Hi Matt. I like your camera. Did you get it for your birthday?
Matt:	Yes, and I'm going out with Dylan this afternoon. He spends most weekends walking around the city taking pictures, and he's asked me to join him.
Girl:	I'd like to try a new activity. My brother Sam plays the guitar, and he thinks I should learn the keyboard. But I'm not good at music. I was thinking about fishing but the lake is too far away.
Matt:	Eva goes fishing, doesn't she?
Girl:	Not anymore. She used to go with her dad, but now she and her sister spend all the time on the boat, and I'm not interested in that.
Matt:	Why don't you speak to Kim? She says there's nothing better than sleeping in a tent and sitting round a fire at night.
Girl:	Hmm … I don't think so. I don't like the idea of sleeping in a tent.
Matt:	Well, how about growing flowers and vegetables? You and Max could start a club together. He also likes being outside in the fresh air and growing things.
Girl:	Hmm … I'll think about it.
Matt:	Or how about joining the theatre club? Ellie is a member. And you were both very good in the school play. What do you think?
Girl:	That's a brilliant idea! I'll call Ellie now.

Now listen again.
That is the end of Part 5. You now have six minutes to write your answers on the answer sheet.
That is the end of the test.

TEST 3   SPEAKING

Part 1

Track 20

Examiner:	Good evening. Can I have your mark sheets, please? I'm Elizabeth Johnson. And this is Tom Clarke. What's your name, Candidate A?
Candidate A:	My name's Kostas Vassilatou.
Examiner:	And what's your name, Candidate B?

[PAUSE FOR YOU TO ANSWER]

| Examiner: | Candidate B, how old are you? |

[PAUSE FOR YOU TO ANSWER]

| Examiner: | Where do you come from, Candidate B? |

[PAUSE FOR YOU TO ANSWER]

Examiner:	Thank you. Candidate A, how old are you?
Candidate A:	I'm thirteen.
Examiner:	Where do you come from?
Candidate A:	I come from Patras in Greece.
Examiner:	Thank you. Now, let's talk about future plans. Candidate A, what are your plans for the weekend?
Candidate A:	On Saturday, it's my birthday so I'm going to go to a concert in the evening. We're going to see our favourite band. I'm really excited!
Examiner:	What are you going to do on Sunday?
Candidate A:	I'm going to play football. My team has an important match in the afternoon.
Examiner:	Candidate B, what plans do you have for next summer?

[PAUSE FOR YOU TO ANSWER]

| Examiner: | Would you like to travel when you are older, Candidate B? |

[PAUSE FOR YOU TO ANSWER]

Examiner:	Now Candidate A, please tell me something about what you would like to study in the future.
Candidate A:	I'm quite good at science and in the future I'd like to go to university to become a doctor.
Examiner:	Now, let's talk about friends. Candidate B, how often do you see your friends?

[PAUSE FOR YOU TO ANSWER]

| Examiner: | What do you like doing with your friends, Candidate B? |

[PAUSE FOR YOU TO ANSWER]

Examiner:	Candidate A, where do your friends live?
Candidate A:	Many of my friends live in the same part of town as me and a few live near the city centre.
Examiner:	When do you see your friends?
Candidate A:	I usually don't see my friends after school because I'm very busy. I have to do my homework and I'm also in a basketball team, so I usually see my friends at the weekend.
Examiner:	Now Candidate B, please tell me something about one of your friends.

[PAUSE FOR YOU TO ANSWER]

| Examiner: | Thank you. |

Part 2

Track 21

Examiner:	Now, in this part of the test you are going to talk together. Here are some pictures that show different types of exercise. Do you like these different types of exercise? Say why or why not. I'll say that again. Do you like these different types of exercise? Say why or why not. All right? Now, talk together.
Candidate A:	I'm quite active and I like exercising, so I think it's fun to go running and swimming. How about you?

[PAUSE FOR YOU TO ANSWER]

Candidate A:	Really? Why do you like dancing?

[PAUSE FOR YOU TO ANSWER]

Candidate A:	Well, I've always liked it. I enjoy being in the water and I think swimming is really good for your health. Some exercises only help some parts of your body, like your legs in cycling, but when you swim you exercise all your body. I think it's a fantastic way to keep fit.
Examiner:	So, Candidate A, why do you like running?
Candidate A:	Because it's great for your health but it also makes me feel good. I can run when I like and where I like, and I don't need any special equipment to do it.
Examiner:	Candidate B, do you think going to the gym is a fun way to exercise?

[PAUSE FOR YOU TO ANSWER]

Examiner:	So Candidate A, which of these types of exercise do you do most often?
Candidate A:	I go running most often. I usually go running with my dad after school, once or twice a week. Then on Sunday morning, I go running with a friend from school.
Examiner:	And you, Candidate B, which of these types of exercise do you do most often?

[PAUSE FOR YOU TO ANSWER]

Examiner:	Thank you.
Examiner:	Now, do you prefer exercising in the week or at the weekend, Candidate B?

[PAUSE FOR YOU TO ANSWER]

Examiner:	Why, Candidate B?

[PAUSE FOR YOU TO ANSWER]

Examiner:	And what about you, Candidate A? Do you prefer exercising in the week or at the weekend?
Candidate A:	I prefer exercising at the weekend. But I know it's good to exercise during the week as well.
Examiner:	Do you prefer exercising with friends or on your own, Candidate A?
Candidate A:	I prefer exercising with friends – or with my dad. You can chat while you're exercising and you don't get lonely.
Examiner:	And you, Candidate B? Do you prefer exercising with friends or on your own?

[PAUSE FOR YOU TO ANSWER]

Examiner:	Why is that, Candidate B?

[PAUSE FOR YOU TO ANSWER]

Examiner:	Thank you. That is the end of the test.

TEST 4   LISTENING

Part 1

Track 22

Key English Test for Schools, Listening
There are five parts to the test. You will hear each piece twice.
We will now stop for a moment.
Please ask any questions now, because you must not speak during the test.
Now look at the instructions for Part 1.
For each question, choose the correct answer.
Look at Question 1.

1   *What is Tom's new Saturday job?*

Girl:	Nice uniform, Tom!
Tom:	Thanks! I had two interviews, one at a shoe shop and one at the sports centre. But as you can see, I'm serving food and drink!
Girl:	I hope I can find a Saturday job, too.
Tom:	Go to the sports centre. I saw an advert that says they need a receptionist.
Girl:	Good idea, thanks!

Now listen again.

2   *What does the girl want for lunch?*

Man:	Are you hungry? I'm making soup for lunch.
Girl:	Soup again! Can't we eat something else, Dad?
Man:	Well, we have fish in the fridge, and there are vegetables, too. We need to use them up before we go on holiday.
Girl:	Hmm ... I don't like fish. I'll have a cheese sandwich. And you and Mum can have the chicken soup!

Now listen again.

3 *Where is the boy's tent?*

Girl: Is that your tent over there by the big tree?

Boy: No, that's Max's tent. Mine is in a really good place. It's next to only one other tent.

Girl: That's good. Is it by the lake?

Boy: No, it's by the river, in that field.

Now listen again.

4 *How does Sue usually communicate with Pablo?*

Penny: Hi Sue. What are you doing? Is that a letter?

Sue: Hi Penny. I'm writing to my friend Pablo. He lives in Chile.

Penny: Cool! Do you always write to him?

Sue: I email him sometimes, but we usually just chat online. This is just a short note. I'm going to send it to him with a magazine. It's got some great articles.

Now listen again.

5 *What did Alex forget to bring to school?*

Mrs Clark: OK, everyone. Please close your books. It's time for the maths test.

Alex: Excuse me, Mrs Clark. Do we need a calculator? I don't have mine.

Mrs Clark: Yes, you do. Please leave only your pen, pencil, ruler and calculator on your desk in front of you. Don't worry if you have forgotten anything. I can lend you anything you need.

Alex: Thank you!

Now listen again.
That is the end of Part 1.

Part 2

Track 23

Now look at Part 2.
For each question, write the correct answer in the gap.
Write one word or a number or a date or a time. Look at questions 6–10 now.
You have ten seconds.
You will hear a teacher talking to a group of students about a student exchange programme.

Woman: The student exchange programme is a great experience. Thirty-four students took part last year and they loved it. I'm sure this year's trip will be just as enjoyable.
The exchange takes place for two weeks. We will travel by plane to the city of Lyon in France – please spell it L-Y-O-N, not L-Y-O-N-S. There we will meet a group of students. Each of you will have a French partner. You will stay with that student in France for one week. Then the French students will come to our school and stay with you in your homes. So you'll be in France from the 4th to the 10th of March. And the Lyon students will be here from the 11th to the 17th of March.
The exchange programme is for students between the ages of 11 and 13. You can take up to £50 with you on the trip to spend as you like. You will have all your meals with your French family, so you won't need to buy food.
If you're interested, speak to me in my office at lunchtime.

Now listen again.
That is the end of Part 2.

Part 3

Track 24

Now look at Part 3.
For each question, choose the correct answer. Look at questions 11–15 now. You have twenty seconds.
You will hear a girl talking on the phone to a staff member at a train station about a train ticket.

Man: Hello, Liverpool train station. How can I help you?

Girl: Hello, I'd like to find out about train times today. Can you help me?

Man: Yes, of course. Where are you travelling?

Girl: Euston Station, in London.

Man: Where are you leaving from?

Girl: Crewe train station.

Man: Let me check for you ... OK, the next train from Liverpool is the 11.13 ... it gets to Crewe at 12.01 p.m. ... and you'll be in Euston at 15.31.

Girl: Thank you. Now, how can I get a ticket? I wanted to buy one online, but the website isn't working.

Man: Well, you can get one from the ticket office at the station or from a ticket machine.

Girl: Great! How much is the ticket?

Man: It's £32.00 for a single, and a return ticket is £41.00.

Girl: I'd like a single ticket, and I have a young person's railcard.

Man: OK, so with the young person's discount, that is £21.10. You can pay now if you like and you can collect your ticket at the station.

Girl: Wonderful!

Man: Can I have your card details, please?

Girl: Yes, sure. I'll just pass the phone to my mum. ...

Now listen again.
That is the end of Part 3.

Part 4

Track 25

Now look at Part 4.
For each question, choose the correct answer.

16 *You will hear a brother and sister talking. Where did the girl leave her glasses?*

Boy: Hurry up, Lucy! We're going to be late for school!

Lucy: Wait! I can't find my glasses. They aren't in my room.

Boy: Have you looked in the living room?

Lucy: Good idea. I'll look now.

Boy: Oh, it's OK. Here they are, next to the sink. You probably left them there while you were putting the dishes in the dishwasher.

Now listen again.

17 *You will hear two friends talking about reading. How does the girl prefer to read?*

Girl: What are you reading?

Boy: It's *Slam*, by Nick Hornby.

Girl: Oh yes, I know it. It was a film, too. I watched it on my laptop. I don't read paper books anymore. I prefer my e-reader because I can have many books on it at once.

Boy: I don't like e-readers. I prefer to turn the pages of a real book!

Now listen again.

18 *You will hear two friends talking in a café. What does the boy want to eat?*

Boy: Sorry I'm late.

Girl: Don't worry. What do you want? Burger? Chicken sandwich?

Boy: No, thanks. I'm not eating meat these days.

Girl: Why not?

Boy: I don't like it. I'm trying to eat healthier. I'll have a pasta salad, but you choose a burger if you want.

Girl: Yes, good idea. Burger and chips. Yum!

Now listen again.

19 *You will hear a girl talking on the phone. Why is she happy?*

Girl: I'm so excited. I can't wait! What time is your flight? ... Mum and I will collect you and your mum and dad from the airport. You'll sleep in my room, and Mum has made the bed in the spare room for Aunt Sue and Uncle Paul. I can't wait for you to meet my friends, and I've planned some great activities for us ...

Now listen again.

20 *You will hear a boy talking to his friend about his summer job. Where was his job?*

Girl: So, Matt, how was your summer? Did you work in the café with your parents, like last year?

Matt: No, I worked with my grandad.

Girl: What did you do?

Matt: I got up at five every morning and fed the chickens and ducks. Then I picked strawberries in the fields all day.

Girl: Wow! You were busy.

Now listen again.
That is the end of Part 4.

Part 5

Track 26

Now look at Part 5.
For each question, choose the correct answer.
Look at Questions 21 to 25 now.
You have 15 seconds.
You will hear Tom talking to his friend Sarah about an international festival at their school. What will each person do for the festival?

Tom: Are you looking forward to the international festival?

Sarah: Yes! We've prepared an area for Max and his band. They need lots of space for their Spanish guitars and drums.

Tom: That's a good idea.

Sarah: There's a table in the hall where we'll put the food and drink. Megan is bringing the lemonade and cola.

Tom: And I'll bring chicken and rice if you like.

Sarah: Thanks, Tom. But you don't need to bring that because Ruby is doing it.

Tom: Well, I'll have my camera with me.

Sarah: That's great! We can put pictures of the festival on the school website.

Tom: Have you heard? Robert's going to organise a place where people can show art from all over the world.

Sarah: What a great idea! That sounds interesting.

Tom: What other entertainment will there be?

Sarah: Well, Denise is going to organise a disco for everyone. She was going to organise a competition, but she changed her mind.

Tom: Sounds good!

Now listen again.
That is the end of Part 5. You now have six minutes to write your answers on the answer sheet.
That is the end of the test.

TEST 4   SPEAKING

Part 1

Track 27

Examiner: Good morning.
Can I have your mark sheets, please?
I'm Barry Alderton and this is Tricia Parker.
What's your name, Candidate A?

| Candidate A: | My name's Alejandro Romero. |
| Examiner: | And what's your name, Candidate B? |

[PAUSE FOR YOU TO ANSWER]

| Examiner: | Candidate B, how old are you? |

[PAUSE FOR YOU TO ANSWER]

| Examiner: | Where do you live, Candidate B? |

[PAUSE FOR YOU TO ANSWER]

Examiner:	Thank you. Candidate A, how old are you?
Candidate A:	I'm thirteen.
Examiner:	Where do you live?
Candidate A:	I live in Madrid too, but I come from Segovia.
Examiner:	Thank you. Now, let's talk about family. Candidate A, what do you enjoy doing with your family?
Candidate A:	I enjoy baking cakes with my grandmother and also going for walks in the forest with my parents and brother.
Examiner:	What do you like about baking?
Candidate A:	My grandmother is the best at baking cakes and biscuits and she's also fun to be with. I learn lots of traditional recipes from her.
Examiner:	Candidate B, what do you like to do at the weekend with your family?

[PAUSE FOR YOU TO ANSWER]

| Examiner: | What do you like to eat when you go out with your family, Candidate B? |

[PAUSE FOR YOU TO ANSWER]

Examiner:	Now Candidate A, please tell me about something interesting that you did with your family recently.
Candidate A:	Last weekend, we went to an old car show. We saw lots of old cars from the past, and some were nearly 100 years old! My dad and I are fans of old cars, so we really enjoyed it.
Examiner:	Now, let's talk about holidays. Candidate B, did you do anything interesting on your holiday?

[PAUSE FOR YOU TO ANSWER]

| Examiner: | What do you like doing on holiday, Candidate B? |

[PAUSE FOR YOU TO ANSWER]

Examiner:	Candidate A, how often do you go on holiday?
Candidate A:	My family and I go maybe two or three times a year.
Examiner:	When do you go on holiday, Candidate A?
Candidate A:	We go for a few weeks during the school summer holidays in August, and then sometimes during the holidays in April and December.

| Examiner: | Now Candidate B, please tell me something about a place that you enjoyed visiting. |

[PAUSE FOR YOU TO ANSWER]

Part 2

Track 28

| Examiner: | Now, in this part of the test you are going to talk together. Here are some pictures that show different types of entertainment. Do you like these different types of entertainment? Say why or why not. I'll say that again. Do you like these different types of entertainment? Say why or why not. All right? Now, talk together. |
| Candidate A: | I think playing video games and chess is fun. How about you? |

[PAUSE FOR YOU TO ANSWER]

| Candidate A: | Why do you think festivals are more fun? |

[PAUSE FOR YOU TO ANSWER]

Candidate A:	Well, I like adventure games where you have to solve a puzzle – they really make you think. I also like playing video games with my friends because it's a fun way to relax.
Examiner:	Candidate A, why do you think playing chess is fun?
Candidate A:	Because you have to think a lot and it takes lots of skill to win a game of chess. And I love winning!
Examiner:	Candidate B, do you think playing board games is interesting?

[PAUSE FOR YOU TO ANSWER]

Examiner:	So Candidate A, which of these types of entertainment do you like the best?
Candidate A:	I like playing chess the best. It isn't only a fun game; it's also good for your brain because you have to think about your next move and how to win.
Examiner:	And you, Candidate B, which of these types of entertainment do you like the best?

[PAUSE FOR YOU TO ANSWER]

| Examiner: | Thank you. Now, do you prefer enjoying yourself indoors or outside, Candidate B? |

[PAUSE FOR YOU TO ANSWER]

| Examiner: | Why, Candidate B? |

[PAUSE FOR YOU TO ANSWER]

Examiner:	And what about you, Candidate A? Do you prefer enjoying yourself indoors or outside?
Candidate A:	I prefer having fun indoors because, for example, you can play games in all kinds of weather. If it rains, you don't need to stop playing.
Examiner:	Do you prefer having fun with friends or family, Candidate A?
Candidate A:	I prefer having fun with my family. My brother enjoys playing chess as well, so we often play with each other – and I usually win!
Examiner:	And you, Candidate B? Do you prefer having fun with friends or family?
[PAUSE FOR YOU TO ANSWER]	
Examiner:	Why, Candidate B?
[PAUSE FOR YOU TO ANSWER]	
Examiner:	Thank you. That is the end of the test.

TEST 5   LISTENING

Part 1

Track 29

Key English Test for Schools, Listening
There are five parts to the test. You will hear each piece twice.
We will now stop for a moment.
Please ask any questions now, because you must not speak during the test.
Now look at the instructions for Part 1.
For each question, choose the correct answer.
Look at Question 1.

1 *Where will Helen meet David?*

David:	Hi Helen. Where are you? Have you finished your homework?
Helen:	Hi David. Yes, I'm at the post office. How about you?
David:	I'm on the bus. I'm going to the swimming pool to meet Tom. Do you want to come?
Helen:	Yes, but I must go home and get my swimming things first. I'll meet you there.

Now listen again.

2 *What time is the girl's new dentist appointment?*

Receptionist:	Good morning, Dr Roberts' office. How can I help you?
Girl:	Hello. I'd like to change my appointment, please. It's at one thirty. Do you have any appointments in the afternoon?

Receptionist:	Hmm ... we're quite busy. Let me see. Dr Roberts is free at two forty-five or five fifteen.
Girl:	Two forty-five is too early, but I can come to the later one. Thanks!

Now listen again.

3 *Where can't the girl take photos?*

Man:	Excuse me, please don't use your camera here.
Girl:	Oh, sorry! I thought I could take photos.
Man:	No, not inside this room with the paintings, but you can in the garden and in the main entrance.
Girl:	OK, thank you.

Now listen again.

4 *How did Richard get to school today?*

Girl:	Happy birthday, Richard! Did you get any nice presents?
Richard:	Thanks! I got a new bike.
Girl:	Great! Can I see it? Did you ride it to school today or did you take the bus?
Richard:	My dad drove me. Why don't you walk home with me after school? I can show you then.
Girl:	OK!

Now listen again.

5 *What will the weather be like this weekend?*

Boy:	Look at the rain!
Girl:	I know! I hope it isn't like this at the weekend for our tennis tournament. I hate playing tennis when it's wet and windy.
Boy:	Well, I saw on the Internet that it will be sunny and warm in the morning but it will get a little cooler in the afternoon.
Girl:	I hope so.

Now listen again.
That is the end of Part 1.

Part 2

Track 30

Now look at Part 2.
For each question, write the correct answer in the gap.
Write one word or a number or a date or a time. Look at questions 6–10 now.
You have ten seconds.
You will hear a chef talking to a group of students about a baking club.

Mr Campbell:	OK, everyone, welcome to the Kids' Baking Club, a club for children aged ten to thirteen. My name's Mr Campbell, that's C-A-M-P-B-E-double L, and I'm going to teach you how to make delicious food! I know you're all excited about getting started, but first let me give

you some information about the class today.

We'll begin in a few minutes, at 10.30 a.m., and we'll finish at 2.30 p.m. We'll stop for lunch at 12. Then, the best part: at around two, we'll try all the cakes you've made! OK, so before we begin, let's wash our hands and prepare the ingredients. Now, I want everyone to get into small groups of three. Each group has their own cooker and space in the kitchen. I need two people from each group to collect the ingredients; one person will go to the fridge and the other to the cupboard. We need flour, butter, milk, eggs and sugar. The third person in the group, could you please turn your oven on to 180 degrees? When you've done all that, I'll tell you what we'll do next. Right, let's start …

Now listen again.
That is the end of Part 2.

Part 3

Track 31

Now look at Part 3.
For each question, choose the correct answer. Look at questions 11–15 now. You have twenty seconds.
You will hear Brian talking to his friend Judy about going to the cinema.

Brian:	Hi Judy. What are you doing this afternoon? Sylvia, Jack and I are going to the cinema. Would you like to come?
Judy:	Hi Brian. I'd love to. What's on?
Brian:	Jack wants to see an action film. I don't mind, but Sylvia doesn't like them. She says they're all the same.
Judy:	I agree with Sylvia. What else is on?
Brian:	Um, there's a comedy … two men go into a zoo one night … people say it's funny… and there's a film about a boy and his dog … the dog dies … and oh, there's a musical and a horror film …
Judy:	Films with singing and dancing are boring, and I don't like scary films, either.
Brian:	Oh, all right. What about the film with the dog?
Judy:	OK, but don't you think the comedy is a better idea? Everyone likes to laugh.
Brian:	Sounds good. Shall we pick you up on our way to the cinema? About three? The film starts at four.
Judy:	No, I've got a piano lesson at half past two and I won't be finished before

quarter past three. I'll meet you at the cinema.

| Brian: | Great! See you later! |

Now listen again.
That is the end of Part 3.

Part 4

Track 32

Now look at Part 4.
For each question, choose the correct answer.
16 *You will hear a girl talking to her friend about her trip. How does she feel now?*

Girl:	Did you have a good journey, Laura?
Laura:	It was long … eight hours and 45 minutes. We left at eleven thirty at night from London.
Girl:	That sounds tiring! Was it really boring?
Laura:	It was OK, and we slept on the plane. But now I can't wait to see the city!

Now listen again.

17 *You will hear a boy talking to a friend on the phone. Why is he excited?*

| Boy: | I'm so excited. Everything is ready. Dad and I went to the supermarket to get the food and drinks. Mum's made a fantastic cake – chocolate, my favourite! My big brother says he'll play some really cool music for us, so we can dance and have fun. And oh, I nearly forgot! Please, please bring your camera! |

Now listen again.

18 *You will hear a mother talking to her son. Where do they decide to put the desk?*

Mike:	What do you think, Mum?
Mum:	Um… if we put the desk next to the door, it will be far from your bookcase. You won't be able to reach your books easily.
Mike:	Why don't we put it in front of the window?
Mum:	No, the heating is there. You'll get too hot. How about between the bookcase and the bed?
Mike:	Yes, good idea!

Now listen again.

19 *You will hear a girl talking to her friend. What does she need to buy?*

Boy:	Are you ready for the race on Saturday?
Girl:	Yes! I'm going to wear my new T-shirt. All I need now are some new socks. I'm going to the sports shop later.
Boy:	What about new trainers? Those look quite old.
Girl:	No! They're my lucky trainers. There's nothing wrong with them!

Now listen again.

20 *You will hear a girl talking to her teacher about school clubs. What is she worried about?*

Girl: Mr Davis, can I still sign up for the singing club?

Mr Davis: Yes, you can. Are you thinking of joining?

Girl: I'm not sure ...

Mr Davis: Are you worried about singing in front of others?

Girl: No, but I already play football and I have a lot of homework this year.

Mr Davis: Come and see how you feel. You might like a change.

Girl: Yes, good idea.

Now listen again.

That is the end of Part 4.

Part 5

Track 33

Now look at Part 5.
For each question, choose the correct answer.
Look at Questions 21 to 25 now.
You have 15 seconds.
You will hear Amber talking to Matt about sports. What sport does each person do?

Amber: Don't forget your racket, Matt. You'll need it for your match this afternoon.

Matt: Yes! It might be useful! Do you like badminton, Amber? You could come and watch.

Amber: Sorry, I can't. I have to be at the pool at three for training.

Matt: Are you meeting Sue there?

Amber: No, Sue doesn't do water sports anymore. She prefers riding her bike in the hills.

Matt: I didn't know that. Hannah was also keen on cycling for a while ... or was it cricket? I forget.

Amber: Cricket?! She hates cricket! She plays hockey now. She wanted to play basketball, but she was too short.

Matt: Your brother plays hockey, doesn't he?

Amber: Who? Paul? No, he loves skateboarding.

Matt: Sorry, did you say skateboarding or snowboarding?

Amber: Skateboarding. It doesn't snow enough to go snowboarding in this country! My brother Jamie is different. He loves the water, like me. He's just bought a new surfboard, and of course, he still goes out on the boat every weekend.

Matt: Cool! We could go to the beach together one Saturday.

Amber: Good idea!

Now listen again.

That is the end of Part 5. You now have six minutes to write your answers on the answer sheet.

That is the end of the test.

TEST 5   SPEAKING

Part 1

Track 34

Examiner: Good afternoon.
Can I have your mark sheets, please?
I'm Angela Burrows and this is Bob Jenkins.
What's your name, Candidate A?

Candidate A: My name's Julia Schmidt.

Examiner: And what's your name, Candidate B?

[PAUSE FOR YOU TO ANSWER]

Examiner: Candidate B, how old are you?

[PAUSE FOR YOU TO ANSWER]

Examiner: Where do you come from, Candidate B?

[PAUSE FOR YOU TO ANSWER]

Examiner: Thank you.
Candidate A, how old are you?

Candidate A: I'm thirteen.

Examiner: Where do you come from?

Candidate A: I come from Vienna in Austria.

Examiner: Thank you.
Now, let's talk about places in a town.
Candidate A, which places in your town are popular with young people?

Candidate A: The parks are popular, and there's also a square in my neighbourhood where a lot of young people go. I like to meet my friends there at the weekend.

Examiner: Why do you like it there?

Candidate A: Because there are some great cafés where we can buy hot chocolate or juice and we can sit and talk.

Examiner: Candidate B, what places are popular with young people?

[PAUSE FOR YOU TO ANSWER]

Examiner: What places would you like in your neighbourhood that you don't have, Candidate B?

[PAUSE FOR YOU TO ANSWER]

Examiner: Now Candidate A, please tell me something about a place you go to when you want to relax.

Candidate A: I'm lucky because there are some lovely parks in my city, so when I want to relax, I go there with my friends for a picnic.

Examiner: Now, let's talk about shopping.
Candidate B, how often do you go shopping?

[PAUSE FOR YOU TO ANSWER]

Examiner:	When do you buy new clothes, Candidate B?

[PAUSE FOR YOU TO ANSWER]

Examiner:	Candidate A, where do you usually go shopping?
Candidate A:	I usually go shopping at department stores, or I go to local shops.
Examiner:	Who do you usually go shopping with?
Candidate A:	I usually go shopping to the supermarket with my mum or dad, but I sometimes go shopping with my friends at the weekend.
Examiner:	Now Candidate B, please tell me about something you bought recently.

[PAUSE FOR YOU TO ANSWER]

Part 2

Track 35

Examiner:	Now, in this part of the test you are going to talk together.
	Here are some pictures that show different types of homes.
	Do you like these different types of homes? Say why or why not. I'll say that again.
	Do you like these different types of homes? Say why or why not.
	All right? Now, talk together.
Candidate A:	I think it would be fun to live on a houseboat or on a farm. How about you?

[PAUSE FOR YOU TO ANSWER]

Candidate A:	Why do you like the house in the mountains?

[PAUSE FOR YOU TO ANSWER]

Candidate A:	Well, I love animals, and if you live on a farm, you can keep different types of animals, like horses and donkeys. Also, a farmhouse is in the countryside, and I love being close to nature.
Examiner:	Candidate A, why do you think living on a houseboat is fun?
Candidate A:	Because it's boring to live in one place all the time. If you live on a houseboat, you can travel to different places whenever you like.
Examiner:	Candidate B, would you like to live in an apartment building like this?

[PAUSE FOR YOU TO ANSWER]

Examiner:	So Candidate A, which of these homes do you like the best?
Candidate A:	Well, if I have to choose between a houseboat and a farmhouse, I will

choose the houseboat because I think it's less work than living on a farm. It's hard work looking after animals all the time – although I love animals.

Examiner:	And you, Candidate B, which of these homes do you like the best?

[PAUSE FOR YOU TO ANSWER]

Examiner:	Thank you.
	Now, would you prefer to live in a big home or a small home, Candidate B?

[PAUSE FOR YOU TO ANSWER]

Examiner:	Why, Candidate B?

[PAUSE FOR YOU TO ANSWER]

Examiner:	And what about you, Candidate A? Would you prefer to live in a big home or a small home?
Candidate A:	I'm not sure, but I think I'd prefer a small home.
Examiner:	Would you prefer to live in a city or in the countryside?
Candidate A:	I'm not sure. I love the country, and I love nature, but in the city you have everything you need there – shops, parks, restaurants, sports centres, cinemas, everything.
Examiner:	And you, Candidate B? Would you prefer to live in a city or in the countryside?

[PAUSE FOR YOU TO ANSWER]

Examiner:	Why is that, Candidate B?

[PAUSE FOR YOU TO ANSWER]

Examiner:	Thank you. That is the end of the test.

TEST 6   LISTENING

Part 1

Track 36

Key English Test for Schools, Listening
There are five parts to the test. You will hear each piece twice.
We will now stop for a moment.
Please ask any questions now, because you must not speak during the test.
Now look at the instructions for Part 1.
For each question, choose the correct answer.
Look at Question 1.

1 *Where did the girl's father see the notebook?*

Girl:	Dad, have you seen my physics notebook anywhere?
Dad:	Look on the desk, next to the laptop.
Girl:	No, it isn't there.
Dad:	Well, it was there last night.
Girl:	And it isn't in my school bag, either.

| Dad: | Maybe Mum put it on the bookshelf when she tidied up this morning. |

Now listen again.

2 *Where did the boy find out about the exhibition?*

Boy:	What are you doing this weekend?
Girl:	I'm going to the opera with my mum. She found tickets online last night. We're going to sit near the stage!
Boy:	Cool! I'm going to an art exhibition. There was a poster for it at school.
Girl:	Oh, yes! I read about it in the newspaper this morning. It looks fun! Have a good time!

Now listen again.

3 *What does Cathy's brother look like?*

Boy:	Great party, Cathy! Is your brother here?
Cathy:	Not yet, but he'll be here soon.
Boy:	Does he look like you and your sister?
Cathy:	Not really. Amanda and I have dark hair and my brother's got dark hair too, but his is short. And he's got light blue eyes. My eyes and Amanda's are dark. I'll introduce you to him when he arrives.

Now listen again.

4 *What would the woman like help with?*

Mum:	Mark, could you help me in the kitchen, please?
Mark:	OK, Mum. Do you want me to do the washing up?
Mum:	No, I've done that. Could you put the plates and glasses in the cupboard? I'm going to start cooking dinner.
Mark:	OK!

Now listen again.

5 *What time is the girl's doctor's appointment?*

Girl:	Dad, can you drive me to my doctor's appointment?
Dad:	Yes, I can, but I don't finish work until 4 p.m. today.
Girl:	Oh no! I need to be there at three forty-five. I'll have to get the bus.
Dad:	Then you'll need to get on the number 390 bus. It goes by our house at twenty-five past three.

Now listen again.
That is the end of Part 1.

Part 2

Track 37

Now look at Part 2.
For each question, write the correct answer in the gap.
Write one word or a number or a date or a time. Look at questions 6–10 now.
You have ten seconds.
You will hear a teacher talking about a special place.

| Woman: | Harbin in China is also known as 'the Ice City'. Every winter, for over 30 years, Harbin has held an ice festival. During this time, tourists come here from all over the world. It takes 7,000 people working together to build the ice city. They cut ice bricks from the frozen Songhua River, which flows through the centre of Harbin, and they make large snow sculptures and full-size buildings. At night, the buildings light up with a rainbow of colours. There are ice castles, ice skyscrapers and ice slides, which are very popular with children. Harbin is in the northeast of China and has an average winter temperature of 17°C below zero – the perfect temperature to build with ice and snow. The freezing temperatures don't keep visitors away. This year over one million people are expected to come. The festival opens on the fifth of January each year and stays open for at least four weeks until spring comes and the Ice City melts away for another year. |

Now listen again.
That is the end of Part 2.

Part 3

Track 38

Now look at Part 3.
For each question, choose the correct answer. Look at questions 11–15 now. You have twenty seconds.
You will hear Cara talking to her friend Tina about a summer holiday.

Cara:	Hey, Tina! Are you still interested in coming on holiday with me this June?
Tina:	Of course, but can we go in July? I can't go earlier because of school, and August is impossible because of my part-time job.
Cara:	Yes, sure, but we must book soon. There's a company called Active Outdoors that a school friend told me about. He went on one of their holidays last year and loved it. There's lots of information on their website.
Tina:	Great!
Cara:	They do different kinds of holidays. There's one by the sea with water sports, and another where you go hiking and learn how to cook outdoors. The one I like best is in the mountains. We can do things like climbing and rafting. What do you think?
Tina:	That sounds amazing! Is it expensive?
Cara:	They've got a special offer at the moment. Normally, the price is three hundred and fifty-five pounds, but if you

book before Friday, it's two hundred and eight-five pounds, so you save seventy pounds.

Tina: What does that include?

Cara: Transport, accommodation and our guide. We only have to pay for food and drink.

Tina: Let's book tonight!

Now listen again.
That is the end of Part 3.

Part 4

Track 39

Now look at Part 4.
For each question, choose the correct answer.
16 *You will hear a man talking on the phone. What is he recommending?*

Man: Here is the information you need. Mr Jones is the best person in the city to help you with a flat. He can find you somewhere nice to live while you're studying in college. He works in the office from Monday to Saturday, but you can contact him any time you want by email.

Now listen again.

17 *You will hear a boy talking to a shop assistant. Why is he upset?*

Boy: Excuse me, I'd like to return this digital camera. I'm not at all happy with it.

Woman: OK, what seems to be the problem?

Boy: Well, I bought it last week but I haven't taken any photos. I charged the battery but it only stays on for a few minutes.

Woman: Oh dear! That's not good. There must be a problem with the battery. Let me take a look …

Now listen again.

18 *You will hear a girl talking to her friend on the phone. What does she need to do?*

Girl: Matt, do you know how I sign up for an afternoon activity?

Matt: Yes, I do. First, you need to choose an activity. Then you go on the school website and complete the online form. You don't need to print the form, but you can if you want a copy. The school office will send you an email about what to do next.

Now listen again.

19 *You will hear two friends talking about holidays. Where did Marcus go?*

Girl: What was your holiday like, Marcus?

Marcus: Fantastic! The best ever!

Girl: Did you go to Scotland again?

Marcus: That's where we usually go, but Mum and Dad changed our plans at the last moment. You'll never guess where we went!

Girl: I don't know… Australia?

Marcus: Wrong! We went to Japan and Korea! But we're going to Scotland again next year.

Now listen again.

20 *You will hear two friends talking about the weekend. Who did the girl visit?*

Harry: Did you enjoy the long weekend, Petra?

Petra: Yes, it was great. I went to Cornwall.

Harry: Great! Your dad's sister lives there, doesn't she?

Petra: No, my mum's. She moved there from Leeds last year. She lives by the sea now, not far from my grandad's place. We had fun on the beach and I even tried surfing!

Now listen again.
That is the end of Part 4.

Part 5

Track 40

Now look at Part 5.
For each question, choose the correct answer.
Look at Questions 21 to 25 now.
You have 15 seconds.
You will hear Emily talking to her friend Duncan about visiting her family in Canada. What gift has Emily's mum bought for each person?

Duncan: So, when are you leaving for Canada, Emily?

Emily: Next week. We're so excited! And Mum has bought everyone gifts. They're in the living room. Come and have a look.

Duncan: … Hey! I'm an Arsenal fan too! Who's the football fan in your family?

Emily: Uncle Zac. I hope he likes the shirt.

Duncan: He will. … And that's very cool!

Emily: It's for Uncle Jim. Photography's his hobby. He takes great pictures.

Duncan: Are these for your granny?

Emily: No, they're for Aunt Maisie. Her hands get cold in the winter, and these will keep them nice and warm.

Duncan: Is the scarf for her, too?

Emily: No, that's for my cousin Simon. Mum also got him this – he doesn't like listening to music with headphones.

Duncan: Lucky Simon! That's a very nice radio. Digital. Was it expensive?

Emily: Yes, it was, and … these earrings were also expensive … but they're beautiful.

Duncan:	For Simon?
Emily:	Don't be silly! They're for my cousin Tamsin.
Duncan:	What about your granny?
Emily:	This. It's about King Richard III. Granny loves history.
Duncan:	Seven hundred pages! Wow! I hope your granny likes reading.

Now listen again.
That is the end of Part 5. You now have six minutes to write your answers on the answer sheet.
That is the end of the test.

TEST 6   SPEAKING

Part 1

Track 41

Examiner:	Good evening. Can I have your mark sheets, please? I'm William Stone. And this is Caroline Morris. What's your name, Candidate A?
Candidate A:	My name's Sakura Ito.
Examiner:	And what's your name, Candidate B?

[PAUSE FOR YOU TO ANSWER]

Examiner:	Candidate B, how old are you?

[PAUSE FOR YOU TO ANSWER]

Examiner:	Where do you live, Candidate B?

[PAUSE FOR YOU TO ANSWER]

Examiner:	Thank you. Candidate A, how old are you?
Candidate A:	I'm thirteen.
Examiner:	Where do you live?
Candidate A:	I also live in Kyoto.
Examiner:	Thank you.
Examiner:	Now, let's talk about favourite subjects. Candidate A, what is your favourite subject at school?
Candidate A:	My favourite subject is geography because I love learning about people and places around the world.
Examiner:	What do you want to study in the future?
Candidate A:	I want to go to university and get a diploma in farm management. My grandparents have a small farm and I want to look after it one day.
Examiner:	Candidate B, what subjects do you enjoy at school?

[PAUSE FOR YOU TO ANSWER]

Examiner:	Would you like to study in Japan or would you like to study in another country, Candidate B?

[PAUSE FOR YOU TO ANSWER]

Examiner:	Now Candidate A, please tell me something about a subject that you don't enjoy at school.
Candidate A:	I don't really enjoy art because I'm not good at drawing and painting, It's a bit boring as well.
Examiner:	Now, let's talk about television. Candidate B, how often do you watch television?

[PAUSE FOR YOU TO ANSWER]

Examiner:	What kind of television programmes do you watch, Candidate B?

[PAUSE FOR YOU TO ANSWER]

Examiner:	Candidate A, do you watch a lot of television?
Candidate A:	No, I don't. I sometimes watch sport at the weekend, or a film, and I also like comedies and quiz shows.
Examiner:	Who do you watch TV with, Candidate A?
Candidate A:	My brother and I watch sport together, and Dad enjoys watching a good film with us too. But I watch quiz shows on my own.
Examiner:	Now Candidate B, please tell me about the sort of television programmes that you don't like.

[PAUSE FOR YOU TO ANSWER]

Part 2

Track 42

Examiner:	Now, in this part of the test you are going to talk together. Here are some pictures that show different ways to travel. Do you like these different ways to travel? Say why or why not. I'll say that again. Do you like these different ways to travel? Say why or why not. All right? Now, talk together.
Candidate A:	I think it's nice to travel by boat and by bike. What do you think?

[PAUSE FOR YOU TO ANSWER]

Candidate A:	Why do you like to travel by train?

[PAUSE FOR YOU TO ANSWER]

Candidate A:	I think it's fun to be on a boat in the sea. It isn't the best way to travel if you want to go somewhere fast, but you can relax. If you want to go to another country, the best way is by plane.

Examiner:	Candidate A, why do you think it is nice to travel by bike?
Candidate A:	Because it's good for your health and it's also good for the environment.
Examiner:	Candidate B, do you think travelling by plane is exciting?

[PAUSE FOR YOU TO ANSWER]

Examiner:	Now, Candidate A, which of these ways to travel do you like the best?
Candidate A:	Well, I will choose travelling by bike because it's better for the world around us, and it's also a good way to keep fit and see different places. But you can't travel everywhere by bike, and sometimes you need to travel by boat, too.
Examiner:	And you, Candidate B, which of these ways to travel do you like the best?

[PAUSE FOR YOU TO ANSWER]

| Examiner: | Thank you. Now, do you prefer travelling on your own or with friends, Candidate B? |

[PAUSE FOR YOU TO ANSWER]

| Examiner: | Why do you like travelling with other people, Candidate B? |

[PAUSE FOR YOU TO ANSWER]

Examiner:	And what about you, Candidate A? Do you prefer travelling on your own or with friends?
Candidate A:	I prefer travelling on my own because I can think.
Examiner:	Do you prefer travelling by bus or by car, Candidate A?
Candidate A:	I prefer travelling by car because you can start your journey any time you want, go where you want to go, and you don't need to stop at bus stops.
Examiner:	And you, Candidate B? Do you prefer travelling by bus or by car?

[PAUSE FOR YOU TO ANSWER]

| Examiner: | Why, Candidate B? |

[PAUSE FOR YOU TO ANSWER]

| Examiner: | Thank you. That is the end of the test. |

TEST 7   LISTENING

Part 1

Track 43

Key English Test for Schools, Listening
There are five parts to the test. You will hear each piece twice.
We will now stop for a moment.

Please ask any questions now, because you must not speak during the test.
Now look at the instructions for Part 1.
For each question, choose the correct answer.
Look at Question 1.

1 *Where is the ticket machine?*

Man:	Excuse me. Could you help me?
Woman:	Yes, of course.
Man:	I'm looking for the ticket machine. Is it near the platform?
Woman:	It's inside the main building. You'll find it next to the seats in the waiting area, opposite the café.

Now listen again.

2 *Where are the two friends going?*

Girl:	Do you have the tickets?
Boy:	Yes, don't worry. They're in my bag. Come on, it starts in ten minutes.
Girl:	Have we got enough money for a programme?
Boy:	Yes, I've got £15. That's enough for a programme. And after the performance, we're meeting some of the actors in the café across the street for a snack.

Now listen again.

3 *How long will the woman stay at the hotel?*

Man:	Good morning, can I help you?
Woman:	Yes, I've booked a room for Friday and Saturday, but I'd like to change that and stay for one more night, please.
Man:	OK, so you want to stay here on Sunday night, too.
Woman:	Yes, that's right.

Now listen again.

4 *Where is the library?*

Girl:	Excuse me, can you tell me the way to the library please?
Man:	Yes. Go along this street past the supermarket and turn left into Church Street. The library is on the right-hand side of the street opposite the bank.
Girl:	Turn left, library on the right. Thank you.
Man:	You're welcome.

Now listen again.

5 *What will they buy?*

Man:	What shall we buy Tonia for passing her exams?
Woman:	How about some clothes?
Man:	We bought her a T-shirt and jeans for her birthday.
Woman:	Hmm ... You're right. Well, she likes photography. How about a book that tells you how to take better pictures?
Man:	Good idea!

Now listen again.
That is the end of Part 1.

Part 2

Track 44

Now look at Part 2.
For each question, write the correct answer in the gap.
Write one word or a number or a date or a time. Look at questions 6–10 now.
You have ten seconds.
You will hear a teacher talking to a group of students about a school event.

Woman:	As you all know, this year our school is taking part in the Great School Clean-up. The event is taking place this Friday, 24th April. Students from secondary schools all over the country will take part. We'll meet in the school playground at 9 a.m.
	We're going to go out into the local area and help clean up rubbish – in the park, around the lake, in the town centre and in the forest. Your teacher will have details of what area each class will clean.
	We are setting off at quarter past nine and we'll spend two hours cleaning. On the day, please wear old clothes and shoes, and bring a pair of thick work or gardening gloves. The school will give you black plastic bags to put the rubbish in. We only have a small number of litter pickers, so if your parents can bring any cleaning equipment to school the day before the clean-up, let your teacher know. Remember we're doing this clean-up to help our environment, so I want everyone to collect as much as they can. Happy cleaning!

Now listen again.
That is the end of Part 2.

Part 3

Track 45

Now look at Part 3.
For each question, choose the correct answer. Look at questions 11–15 now. You have twenty seconds.
You will hear Sofia talking to her friend Oliver about their school project.

Sofia:	Oliver, we must talk about our project. Mr Barron doesn't want us to write about just one thing. First, we have to find out how many students in school speak more than one language.
Oliver:	Yes, and also what level their English is. Anything else?
Sofia:	I don't think so.
Oliver:	We have to speak to a lot of people!
Sofia:	That's true, but I'm sure half of them speak only one language.
Oliver:	That's still a lot of students, and we've only got a week to find and speak to them.
Sofia:	OK, let's find out how many students there are in the school in total. Then we can work out how many speak two or more languages. Maybe there's a list somewhere, like in the library?
Oliver:	Why don't we ask the school office? On my first day here, my teacher gave me a form to complete. One question was about what languages I spoke. Everyone has to complete a form like that.
Sofia:	Good idea. I'll phone now and make an appointment to see Mrs Davis after class.
Oliver:	OK, and I'll start writing notes.

Now listen again.
That is the end of Part 3.

Part 4

Track 46

Now look at Part 4.
For each question, choose the correct answer.
16 *You will hear a boy talking on the phone. What is he planning to do?*

Boy:	Robert, I can only go on Sunday. I've got football practice on Saturday. I don't mind if we miss Katie Ray, but I really want to hear The Rain! We can get something to eat at the stadium, but bring an umbrella. Oh, and wear something warm. I'll get the tickets online tonight and you can pay me there.

Now listen again.

17 *You will hear a girl talking to her friend about food. What can't she eat?*

Boy:	What are you going to have?
Girl:	Well, there are only three things on the menu and I'm tired of eating salad.
Boy:	Why don't you try the grilled mushrooms or the chicken? They look delicious.
Girl:	I'm a vegetarian, remember!
Boy:	Oh, I keep forgetting. Well, what about the cheese omelette?
Girl:	Yes, I might get that.

Now listen again.

18 *You will hear a boy talking to his friend. What is he worried about?*

Girl:	So, are you ready for the interview?
Boy:	Yes, I think so. I practised answering questions with my dad at the weekend so I'm quite confident.

| Girl: | That was a good idea! |
| Boy: | I'm just worried about getting lost. I have to go by bus because Mum is working and can't drive me. |

Now listen again.

19 *You will hear a girl talking to her friend. Why didn't she go to the swimming pool?*

| Boy: | I didn't see you at the swimming pool on Wednesday. Were you ill? |
| Girl: | I was fine, but I had a project for school, and I had to look for some books at the library. When I left, it was too late to do anything else, so I decided to go home for dinner. |

Now listen again.

20 *You will hear two friends talking about a camping trip. What did the girl see?*

Boy:	So, what was the camping trip like?
Girl:	Fantastic! But it's really different camping in autumn.
Boy:	Yes, for a start, it's much cooler.
Girl:	But the countryside is so beautiful. There aren't many flowers, but the leaves are amazing! Red, yellow, orange ...
Boy:	Yes, and the fields are wet and muddy.

Now listen again.
That is the end of Part 4.

Part 5

Track 47

Now look at Part 5.
For each question, choose the correct answer.
Look at Questions 21 to 25 now.
You have 15 seconds.
You will hear Harry talking to Eleanor about her trip.
What was the weather like on each day?

Harry:	Did you have a good time on your trip, Eleanor?
Eleanor:	We had a great time, but the weather didn't start out very nice on Monday.
Harry:	Oh, no! Did it rain?
Eleanor:	No, but the sky was grey and the sun didn't come out all day.
Harry:	How about on Tuesday? Was it better?
Eleanor:	Not really. The temperature was very low, so I wore a coat all day. We wanted to take a boat ride but instead we went to a museum.
Harry:	What about Wednesday? It was a beautiful sunny day here.
Eleanor:	It was the same there! The temperature went up and it was warm, and we finally went on the boat ride.
Harry:	Oh great!
Eleanor:	Yes, and on Thursday the temperature went up even more, so we spent the day on the beach.

Harry:	Did it stay hot?
Eleanor:	No, unfortunately. On Friday, the wind began to blow.
Harry:	Did you have a storm?
Eleanor:	No, but we couldn't go sailing. It was too dangerous. Then the next day, it rained and there was thunder and lightning. That was Saturday. It was really exciting!
Harry:	The only weather you didn't have was snow!

Now listen again.
That is the end of Part 5. You now have six minutes to write your answers on the answer sheet.
That is the end of the test.

TEST 7   SPEAKING

Part 1

Track 48

Examiner:	Good morning. Can I have your mark sheets, please? I'm Monica Taylor. And this is Sam Chapman. What's your name, Candidate A?
Candidate A:	My name's Jose Fernandes.
Examiner:	And what's your name, Candidate B?

[PAUSE FOR YOU TO ANSWER]

| Examiner: | Candidate B, how old are you? |

[PAUSE FOR YOU TO ANSWER]

| Examiner: | Where do you come from, Candidate B? |

[PAUSE FOR YOU TO ANSWER]

Examiner:	Thank you. Candidate A, how old are you?
Candidate A:	I'm thirteen.
Examiner:	Where do you come from?
Candidate A:	I come from Rio de Janeiro in Brazil.
Examiner:	Thank you. Now, let's talk about hobbies. Candidate A, what hobbies do you have?
Candidate A:	I like drawing and I'm a big fan of Japanese art, so I like drawing manga-style cartoons in my spare time.
Examiner:	Why do you like drawing?
Candidate A:	Because it's great to make something new. I like using my imagination. It also helps me to relax and forget about things that worry me, like my schoolwork.
Examiner:	Candidate B, what kinds of hobbies are popular with your friends?

[PAUSE FOR YOU TO ANSWER]

Examiner:	What hobbies would you like to try, Candidate B?

[PAUSE FOR YOU TO ANSWER]

Examiner:	Now Candidate A, please tell me something about a hobby you wouldn't like to try.
Candidate A:	Well, I wouldn't like to dance or sing. I'm a shy person and I don't like performing in front of other people.
Examiner:	Now, let's talk about jobs. Candidate B, what kind of weekend jobs are popular with young people?

[PAUSE FOR YOU TO ANSWER]

Examiner:	What job would you like to do, Candidate B?

[PAUSE FOR YOU TO ANSWER]

Examiner:	Candidate A, would you like to have your own business in the future?
Candidate A:	Yes, I think so because it would be nice to be a boss, but it's also lots of hard work.
Examiner:	What type of business would you have?
Candidate A:	I think I'd like a photography business. I'm quite good at taking photos with my camera, so I could take photos of people at different special events.
Examiner:	Now Candidate B, please tell me something about a job you wouldn't want to do.

[PAUSE FOR YOU TO ANSWER]

Part 2

Track 49

Examiner:	Now, in this part of the test you are going to talk together. Here are some pictures that show different ways to stay healthy. Do you like these different ways to stay healthy? Say why or why not. I'll say that again. Do you like these different ways to stay healthy? Say why or why not. All right? Now, talk together.
Candidate A:	I think it's very important to exercise often, eat fresh food and drink lots of water. How about you?

[PAUSE FOR YOU TO ANSWER]

Candidate A:	Why do you think sleep is so important?

[PAUSE FOR YOU TO ANSWER]

Candidate A:	I think it's good for us because it helps us not to get ill very often. It helps us relax and it makes our body stronger. When I have lots of homework or when I'm studying for exams, I take regular breaks and do some exercise. It helps me think and remember better.
Examiner:	Candidate A, how do you think reading helps you keep healthy?
Candidate A:	Because it helps you relax. It's much better for you than watching TV or playing video games, which are bad for you if you look at a screen for many hours.
Examiner:	Candidate B, do you think walking is good for you?

[PAUSE FOR YOU TO ANSWER]

Examiner:	So Candidate A, which of these ways to stay healthy do you think is the best?
Candidate A:	I think that exercising is the best way to stay healthy because it's good for your body and your mind. You stay strong and you don't get so tired.
Examiner:	And you, Candidate B, which of these ways to stay healthy do you think is the best?

[PAUSE FOR YOU TO ANSWER]

Examiner:	Thank you. Now, Candidate B, what kind of food do you think is good for you?

[PAUSE FOR YOU TO ANSWER]

Examiner:	Which ones do you like, Candidate B?

[PAUSE FOR YOU TO ANSWER]

Examiner:	And what about you, Candidate A? What kind of food do you think is good for you?
Candidate A:	Fruit, vegetables, fish, milk, cheese, and not a lot of meat. I eat lots of fruit every day.
Examiner:	Which fruit do you like, Candidate A?
Candidate A:	I like all fruit, but I don't like many vegetables. The only vegetables I like are peas and tomatoes.
Examiner:	Do you like waking up early or late, Candidate A?
Candidate A:	I prefer waking up late because I usually chat to my friends late at night. So it's difficult to wake up early in the mornings.
Examiner:	And you, Candidate B? Do you like waking up early or late?

[PAUSE FOR YOU TO ANSWER]

Examiner:	Why is that, Candidate B?

[PAUSE FOR YOU TO ANSWER]

Examiner: Thank you. That is the end of the test.

TEST 8   LISTENING

Part 1

Track 50

Key English Test for Schools, Listening.
There are five parts to the test. You will hear each piece twice.
We will now stop for a moment.
Please ask any questions now, because you must not speak during the test.
Now look at the instructions for Part 1.
For each question, choose the correct answer.
Look at Question 1.

1 *What time is Derek's train?*

Woman: Hi Derek. What are you doing here? Did you miss your train?

Derek: Well, the train at five past five was full.

Woman: But the next one is at ten past six! You're going to get home very late!

Derek: It's OK. They've put on another train at twenty to six because of the long weekend.

Woman: So there's one before ten past six?

Derek: Yes.

Now listen again.

2 *How will they get to the dentist's office?*

Mum: Oh no, we're going to be late!

Boy: What time is my appointment, Mum?

Mum: At four. Even if we start walking fast now, we'll still be late. We'd better phone for a taxi – or take a bus.

Boy: Look, there's a bus stop over there.

Mum: What time is the next bus, darling?

Boy: Um ... not for another 25 minutes.

Mum: I'll make a call, then.

Now listen again.

3 *What does the boy have to buy?*

Girl: Why are you going shopping with your mum?

Boy: My aunt is getting married next week and I need smart clothes for the wedding.

Girl: What are you going to wear?

Boy: A suit. We bought one on Saturday, and we also got a tie, but I need a new shirt. My blue one doesn't look good with the new tie.

Now listen again.

4 *What do they need from the supermarket?*

Woman: What do we need for the burgers? Do we have enough meat?

Man: Yes, we have that at home. But we must get some bread.

Woman: We need some more things for the burgers, don't we? What about cheese and tomatoes?

Man: Good idea, but we have enough at home.

Now listen again.

5 *What does Rachel's mother suggest?*

Rachel: Mum, my head hurts. Can I take something for the pain? Have we got any aspirin?

Mum: I don't think you need any painkillers, Rachel. You just need to get some exercise. Go out for a walk or play basketball with your friends.

Rachel: Oh, Mum! I just want to rest.

Mum: You've got a headache because you spend too many hours playing video games.

Now listen again.
That is the end of Part 1.

Part 2

Track 51

Now look at Part 2.
For each question, write the correct answer in the gap.
Write one word or a number or a date or a time. Look at questions 6–10 now.
You have ten seconds.
You will hear a student giving a talk about the world's tallest building.

Girl: The Burj Khalifa in Dubai in the United Arab Emirates is the world's tallest building. It's more than half a mile tall; that's over 800 metres. It's taller than any other building in the world, but it has one big problem – its windows get dirty. Keeping all the windows on the building clean isn't an easy job. It needs a team of 15 men. And not everyone can do it. The cleaners have to work hundreds of metres above the ground, so they mustn't be scared of being high up. When they are cleaning the building's 24,000 windows they have to be very careful. It's very windy, and the wind is the strongest at the top of the building. The team must work for three months to clean all of the windows of the Burj Khalifa. It's a dangerous but exciting job. And what happens when they've finished? They have to start all over again!

Now listen again.
That is the end of Part 2.

Part 3

Track 52

Now look at Part 3.
For each question, choose the correct answer. Look at questions 11–15 now. You have twenty seconds.

You will hear Sam talking to her friend Ivan about joining a gym.

Sam:	So, did you join a gym?
Ivan:	Yes, I did. It's got great equipment.
Sam:	Is it the gym next to the library?
Ivan:	No, it's the building next to the park, opposite Smith's department store.
Sam:	Oh yes, I know it. I see a lot of people going there. It looks really big. I heard it's expensive.
Ivan:	It's forty pounds a month.
Sam:	Forty pounds! That's too expensive for me.
Ivan:	But you can go there every day if you want. I go three times a week, so that's about £3 every time I go. And if you pay for the year when you join, it's £400, so you save money.
Sam:	What do they have there?
Ivan:	There's a juice bar, which is really healthy, but a lot of people prefer the café next to the department store. And there's a great swimming pool.
Sam:	Ooh, I love swimming.
Ivan:	So, do you think you'll join the gym?
Sam:	I'm not sure. I run in the park every afternoon, I go swimming at the sports centre on Saturdays and I play tennis there twice a week.
Ivan:	Wow! You have a busy schedule!

Now listen again.
That is the end of Part 3.

Part 4

Track 53

Now look at Part 4.
For each question, choose the correct answer.

16 *You will hear two friends talking about a pair of sunglasses. What doesn't the girl like about them?*

Boy:	Nice sunglasses. Are they new?
Girl:	Yes, I got them last week, but now I'm not so sure about them. I don't think the shape suits my face.
Boy:	Well, they're bigger than your old ones. The colour is nice, though.
Girl:	Yes, I like the colour. That's why I bought them.

Now listen again

17 *You will hear a boy talking about his journey to school this morning. How did he get there?*

Girl:	Where were you this morning, Tom? I didn't see you outside in the school playground.
Boy:	I was late. I left home on time, but I had to walk to my grandmother's house first. I left my maths book there last night. So my grandad had to drive me to school.

Girl:	Oh! So you missed the usual bus as well.

Now listen again.

18 *You will hear a girl talking to her friend about a new mobile phone. Why did she buy it?*

Boy:	So, you finally got a new phone, Julia!
Julia:	Yes. Do you like it?
Boy:	Cool!
Julia:	Thanks! It wasn't cheap, but I paid for it with money from my Saturday job. It takes brilliant photos, and the battery lasts for hours and hours.
Boy:	There was a problem with your old phone, wasn't there?
Julia:	Yeah. I couldn't switch it on, and they couldn't repair it.

Now listen again.

19 *You will hear a boy talking to his friend about an accident. What happened?*

Girl:	What happened to your hand?
Boy:	I hurt my finger while I was fishing with my dad.
Girl:	Is it broken?
Boy:	No, it isn't, but I cut it quite badly. I have to wear this bandage for a week. I also have a small cut on my right arm.

Now listen again.

20 *You will hear a girl talking to her friend about a party. What does she need help with?*

Boy:	Are you ready for the party?
Girl:	Well, Mum and I have made the food. It's in the kitchen with the drinks. I just need to put everything on the table.
Boy:	The decorations look great.
Girl:	Thanks. Fred helped me to put up the balloons.
Boy:	What about the music?
Girl:	Dan's organising that, but I can't carry everything out from the kitchen by myself.
Boy:	Let's do it together!

Now listen again.
That is the end of Part 4.

Part 5

Track 54

Now look at Part 5.
For each question, choose the correct answer.
Look at Questions 21 to 25 now.
You have 15 seconds.
You will hear Bella talking to a school advisor about different subjects. What does each person suggest that she study at university?

Advisor:	Hello, Bella! How can I help?
Bella:	Well, I want to go to university but I don't know what subject to study. I like

Advisor:	learning about life in the past, but my parents don't agree.
Advisor:	OK. What do they say?
Bella:	Dad wants me to be a doctor. He's a dentist. It's a well-paid job, so he thinks I should do something where I can earn lots of money.
Advisor:	What about your mum?
Bella:	Mum says I'm good with numbers, so I should study maths. But I find it boring.
Advisor:	I see. Maybe you could study a subject related to a hobby.
Bella:	Well, I play the piano ...
Advisor:	That's interesting.
Bella:	My brother thinks I should become a musician, but I don't think it could be my job.
Advisor:	Sometimes a hobby can become a job!
Bella:	Good point ... I also enjoy drawing and painting. I work in a gallery in town part time. The manager there likes my paintings. She says I should do that as my career.
Advisor:	It's great to do something you enjoy.
Bella:	Grandad says that, too. He was a teacher and he loved teaching, but I don't want to do that. He and I enjoy learning about different countries. He suggested I study something like that. Then maybe I could get a job travelling the world ...
Advisor:	Well, let's discuss some of the possibilities a bit more ...

Now listen again.
That is the end of Part 5. You now have six minutes to write your answers on the answer sheet.
That is the end of the test.

TEST 8   SPEAKING

Part 1

Track 55

Examiner:	Good afternoon. Can I have your mark sheets, please? I'm James Bennett. And this is Ursula Brown. What's your name, Candidate A?
Candidate A:	My name's Andrea Koch.
Examiner:	And what's your name, Candidate B?
[PAUSE FOR YOU TO ANSWER]	
Examiner:	Candidate B, how old are you?
[PAUSE FOR YOU TO ANSWER]	
Examiner:	Where do you live, Candidate B?
[PAUSE FOR YOU TO ANSWER]	
Examiner:	Thank you. Candidate A, how old are you?

Candidate A:	I'm thirteen.
Examiner:	Where do you live?
Candidate A:	I live in Villach.
Examiner:	Thank you. Now, let's talk about music. Candidate A, what is your favourite type of music?
Candidate A:	I'm a big fan of rock music. I often listen to rock on my phone on the way to school.
Examiner:	Why do you like rock?
Candidate A:	Because it has a good rhythm. Rock music is exciting; it never sounds boring.
Examiner:	Candidate B, what kind of music do your friends listen to?
[PAUSE FOR YOU TO ANSWER]	
Examiner:	What kind of music do you often listen to, Candidate B?
[PAUSE FOR YOU TO ANSWER]	
Examiner:	Now Candidate A, please tell me something about music that you don't like.
Candidate A:	I'm not a big fan of hip hop because I think they talk or sing too fast, and most of the time it just sounds like shouting to me.
Examiner:	Now, let's talk about your home. Candidate B, what is your favourite room in your home?
[PAUSE FOR YOU TO ANSWER]	
Examiner:	What do you like best about your bedroom, Candidate B?
[PAUSE FOR YOU TO ANSWER]	
Examiner:	Candidate A, where do you and your family spend most of your time at home?
Candidate A:	In the evenings, we often spend our time in the living room. We read books, watch TV and sometimes play board games together.
Examiner:	What is your bedroom like, Candidate A?
Candidate A:	It's quite big and it has a wardrobe for my clothes. My desk is in front of the window so it's nice and light while I'm doing my homework. I've got lots of posters on the wall, too.
Examiner:	Now Candidate B, please tell me about something you don't like about your home.
[PAUSE FOR YOU TO ANSWER]	

Part 2

Track 56

Examiner:	Now, in this part of the test you are going to talk together.

Here are some pictures that show different types of weather.
Do you like these different types of weather? Say why or why not. I'll say that again.
Do you like these different types of weather? Say why or why not.
All right? Now, talk together.

Candidate A: I like it when it's hot and sunny because then you can sit outside and enjoy trees and flowers. But it's also exciting when there's a thunderstorm. What type of weather do you like?

[PAUSE FOR YOU TO ANSWER]

Candidate A: Why do you like cool and windy weather?

[PAUSE FOR YOU TO ANSWER]

Candidate A: I think it's fun to watch them from my bedroom window. I like to see all the bright flashes from the lightning and hear the loud noise of the thunder.

Examiner: Candidate A, do you enjoy snowy weather?

Candidate A: Well, I like to see the snow because it makes everything look very beautiful, but I don't like going out in the snow very much. It's too cold!

Examiner: Candidate B, how do you feel about rainy weather?

[PAUSE FOR YOU TO ANSWER]

Examiner: So Candidate A, which of these types of weather do you like best?

Candidate A: I like hot sunny weather the best because it makes me feel happy and it makes everything in my city look beautiful. The mountains near Villach are lovely in the summer.

Examiner: And you, Candidate B, which of these types of weather do you like best?

[PAUSE FOR YOU TO ANSWER]

Examiner: Thank you.

Examiner: Now, do you prefer the summer or the winter, Candidate B?

[PAUSE FOR YOU TO ANSWER]

Examiner: Why, Candidate B?

[PAUSE FOR YOU TO ANSWER]

Examiner: And what about you, Candidate A? Do you prefer the summer or the winter?

Candidate A: I prefer the summer because I love going to the lakes with my friends and swimming or windsurfing.

Examiner: Do you prefer to visit hot countries or cold countries on holiday, Candidate A?

Candidate A: I prefer to visit hot countries because you don't need to take lots of clothes with you. You just need T-shirts and shorts, and a pair of sunglasses. And you can go swimming in the sea and surfing!

Examiner: And you, Candidate B? Do you prefer to visit hot countries or cold countries on holiday?

[PAUSE FOR YOU TO ANSWER]

Examiner: Thank you. That is the end of the test.

Sample answer sheets

Cambridge Assessment
English

Candidate Name		Candidate Number	

Centre Name		Centre Number	

Examination Title		Examination Details	

Candidate Signature		Assessment Date	

Supervisor: If the candidate is ABSENT or has WITHDRAWN shade here ○

Key for Schools Reading and Writing Candidate Answer Sheet

Instructions
Use a PENCIL (B or HB).
Rub out any answer you want to change with an eraser.

For Parts 1, 2, 3 and 4:
Mark ONE letter for each answer.
For example: If you think A is the right answer to the question, mark your answer sheet like this:

For Part 5:
Write your answers clearly in the spaces next to the numbers (25 to 30) like this:

`0 | E N G L I S H`

Write your answers in CAPITAL LETTERS.

Part 1			Part 2			Part 3			Part 4		
1	A B C ○ ○ ○		7	A B C ○ ○ ○		14	A B C ○ ○ ○		19	A B C ○ ○ ○	
2	A B C ○ ○ ○		8	A B C ○ ○ ○		15	A B C ○ ○ ○		20	A B C ○ ○ ○	
3	A B C ○ ○ ○		9	A B C ○ ○ ○		16	A B C ○ ○ ○		21	A B C ○ ○ ○	
4	A B C ○ ○ ○		10	A B C ○ ○ ○		17	A B C ○ ○ ○		22	A B C ○ ○ ○	
5	A B C ○ ○ ○		11	A B C ○ ○ ○		18	A B C ○ ○ ○		23	A B C ○ ○ ○	
6	A B C ○ ○ ○		12	A B C ○ ○ ○					24	A B C ○ ○ ○	
			13	A B C ○ ○ ○							

Part 5		Do not write below here			Do not write below here
25		25 1 0 ○ ○	28		28 1 0 ○ ○
26		26 1 0 ○ ○	29		29 1 0 ○ ○
27		27 1 0 ○ ○	30		30 1 0 ○ ○

Put your answers to Writing Parts 6 and 7 on the separate Answer Sheet

Reproduced with permission of Cambridge Assessment English © copyright UCLES 2019.

Sample answer sheet

12734

Cambridge Assessment
English

Candidate Name		Candidate Number	

Centre Name		Centre Number	

Examination Title		Examination Details	

Candidate Signature		Assessment Date	

Supervisor: If the candidate is ABSENT or has WITHDRAWN shade here ○

Key for Schools Writing

Candidate Answer Sheet for Parts 6 and 7

INSTRUCTIONS TO CANDIDATES

Make sure that your name and candidate number are on this sheet.

Write your answers to Writing Parts 6 and 7 on the other side of this sheet.

Use a pencil.

You **must** write within the grey lines.

Do **not** write on the bar codes.

12734

12734

Part 6: Write your answer below.

Part 7: Write your answer below.

Examiner's Use Only

Part 6	C	O	L

Part 7	C	O	L

12734

198

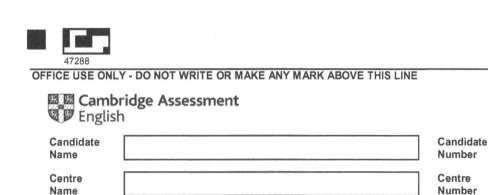

47288

Cambridge Assessment
English

Candidate Name		Candidate Number	
Centre Name		Centre Number	
Examination Title		Examination Details	
Candidate Signature		Assessment Date	

Supervisor: If the candidate is ABSENT or has WITHDRAWN shade here ○

Key for Schools Listening Candidate Answer Sheet

Instructions

Use a PENCIL (B or HB).
Rub out any answer you want to change with an eraser.

For Parts 1, 3, 4 and 5:
Mark ONE letter for each answer.
For example: If you think A is the right answer to the question, mark your answer sheet like this:

For Part 2:
Write your answers clearly in the spaces next to the numbers (6 to 10) like this:

Write your answers in CAPITAL LETTERS.

Part 1

	A	B	C
1	○	○	○
2	○	○	○
3	○	○	○
4	○	○	○
5	○	○	○

Part 2

		Do not write below here
6		6 1 0 ○ ○
7		7 1 0 ○ ○
8		8 1 0 ○ ○
9		9 1 0 ○ ○
10		10 1 0 ○ ○

Part 3

	A	B	C
11	○	○	○
12	○	○	○
13	○	○	○
14	○	○	○
15	○	○	○

Part 4

	A	B	C
16	○	○	○
17	○	○	○
18	○	○	○
19	○	○	○
20	○	○	○

Part 5

	A	B	C	D	E	F	G	H
21	○	○	○	○	○	○	○	○
22	○	○	○	○	○	○	○	○
23	○	○	○	○	○	○	○	○
24	○	○	○	○	○	○	○	○
25	○	○	○	○	○	○	○	○

47288

Answer key for the Reading and Listening

This is the Answer key for the Reading and Listening parts of Tests 1-8.

TEST 1

Reading

Part 1
1 C
2 B
3 C
4 A
5 B
6 A

Part 2
7 C
8 A
9 B
10 A
11 B
12 C
13 A

Part 3
14 C
15 C
16 A
17 A
18 B

Part 4
19 C
20 A
21 B
22 A
23 C
24 B

Part 5
25 about
26 as
27 too
28 you
29 and
30 are

Listening

Part 1
1 B
2 C
3 C
4 A
5 B

Part 2
6 8 p.m. / eight p.m.
7 midnight / twelve a.m. / 12 a.m.
8 20/twenty
9 £2.00
10 020 876 9719

Part 3
11 C
12 C
13 B
14 A
15 A

Part 4
16 A
17 B
18 A
19 C
20 B

Part 5
21 H
22 G
23 C
24 F
25 B

TEST 2

Reading

Part 1
1 B
2 C
3 A
4 B
5 C
6 A

Part 2
7 A
8 B
9 A
10 C
11 A
12 C
13 A

Part 3
14 B
15 A
16 C
17 A
18 B

Part 4
19 C
20 A
21 A
22 B
23 C
24 C

Part 5
25 on
26 to
27 about
28 were/are
29 do
30 or

Listening

Part 1
1 C
2 B
3 A
4 C
5 C

Part 2
6 10/ten
7 Ernest
8 1.99
9 50,000
10 5.30 / five thirty / half past five

Part 3
11 A
12 B
13 C
14 C
15 A

Part 4
16 B
17 A
18 B
19 C
20 A

Part 5
21 A
22 F
23 D
24 H
25 C

TEST 3

Reading

Part 1
1 A
2 C
3 B
4 C
5 B
6 C

Part 2
7 C
8 A
9 B
10 A
11 C
12 B
13 C

Part 3
14 C
15 B
16 C
17 A
18 C

Part 4
19 B
20 C
21 A
22 B
23 C
24 A

Part 5
25 and
26 is
27 to/till/until
28 you
29 Does
30 the

Listening

Part 1
1 C
2 B
3 A
4 B
5 C

Part 2
6 7.30
7 Pankhurst
8 Monday
9 3/three
10 hat

Part 3
11 B
12 A
13 A
14 C
15 A

Part 4
16 B
17 C
18 A
19 B
20 C

Part 5
21 B
22 H
23 D
24 A
25 C

TEST 4

Reading

Part 1
1 A
2 B
3 B
4 C
5 A
6 B

Part 2
7 A
8 B
9 C
10 A
11 C
12 B
13 A

Part 3
14 C
15 B
16 B
17 C
18 A

Part 4
19 B
20 A
21 C
22 B
23 C
24 B

Part 5
25 my
26 any
27 the
28 to
29 of
30 lot

Listening

Part 1
1 A
2 C
3 B
4 C
5 A

Part 2
6 Lyon
7 4th/fourth
8 11/eleven
9 50
10 family

Part 3
11 B
12 B
13 C
14 A
15 A

Part 4
16 B
17 C
18 A
19 B
20 B

Part 5
21 G
22 E
23 H
24 F
25 D

TEST 5

Reading

Part 1
1 C
2 C
3 A
4 B
5 A
6 C

Part 2
7 B
8 C
9 C
10 A
11 B
12 C
13 A

Part 3
14 B
15 C
16 A
17 B
18 A

Part 4
19 C
20 A
21 B
22 C
23 A
24 B

Part 5
25 with
26 Do
27 a
28 from
29 I
30 if/whether

Listening

Part 1
1 C
2 C
3 A
4 B
5 C

Part 2
6 Campbell
7 10.30
8 3/three
9 milk
10 180

Part 3
11 C
12 C
13 A
14 B
15 A

Part 4
16 B
17 B
18 A
19 B
20 C

Part 5
21 C
22 A
23 F
24 E
25 G

TEST 6

Reading

Part 1
1 B
2 C
3 C
4 B
5 C
6 A

Part 2
7 B
8 C
9 A
10 B
11 B
12 A
13 C

Part 3
14 B
15 C
16 A
17 C
18 A

Part 4
19 B
20 C
21 A
22 B
23 A
24 C

Part 5
25 or
26 if
27 have
28 on
29 him
30 goes

Listening

Part 1
1 A
2 B
3 B
4 C
5 B

Part 2
6 6,700
7 river
8 17
9 1/one
10 5th

Part 3
11 B
12 C
13 B
14 A
15 C

Part 4
16 A
17 B
18 A
19 B
20 C

Part 5
21 C
22 H
23 B
24 A
25 G

TEST 7

Reading

Part 1
1 B
2 C
3 A
4 B
5 B
6 C

Part 2
7 C
8 A
9 B
10 B
11 C
12 A
13 A

Part 3
14 B
15 A
16 C
17 A
18 C

Part 4
19 C
20 A
21 B
22 C
23 A
24 B

Part 5
25 not
26 and/so
27 a
28 for
29 when
30 you

Listening

Part 1
1 C
2 A
3 C
4 A
5 B

Part 2
6 24/24th
7 lake
8 2/two
9 old
10 bags

Part 3
11 B
12 C
13 A
14 B
15 B

Part 4
16 C
17 B
18 A
19 C
20 A

Part 5
21 H
22 A
23 D
24 G
25 B

TEST 8

Reading

Part1
1 A
2 B
3 B
4 C
5 A
6 B

Part 2
7 B
8 C
9 A
10 C
11 A
12 B
13 A

Part 3
14 B
15 C
16 A
17 C
18 C

Part 4
19 A
20 C
21 B
22 C
23 A
24 A

Part 5
25 at
26 it
27 going
28 never
29 a/the
30 too

Listening

Part 1
1 B
2 C
3 A
4 A
5 B

Part 2
6 dirty
7 15/fifteen
8 24,000
9 3/three
10 exciting

Part 3
11 A
12 B
13 C
14 C
15 A

Part 4
16 A
17 C
18 B
19 B
20 A

Part 5
21 D
22 B
23 F
24 A
25 G

Model answers for Writing

These are the model answers for the Writing parts of Tests 1–8.

Test 1

Writing Part 6

Question 31

> Hi Ben,
> Let's go to the cinema on Saturday. I'd like to go to the one in town. We can travel there on the bus.

Writing Part 7

Question 32

One day, Mike and Ian went snowboarding in the mountains. Mike had an accident. He hurt his head on a tree. Ian used his mobile phone to call for an ambulance. The ambulance came and took Mike to hospital. Ian also went in the ambulance. Mike is better now.

Test 2

Writing Part 6

Question 31

> Hi Alex,
> Let's meet at 10 a.m. on Saturday at my house Please bring some food and water. I'll bring some bread, a tin of beans and a bottle of orange juice. We can go walking in the forest.

Writing Part 7

Question 32

James was bored at home so he phoned his friend. They went to the park. There, they played with a ball and had a lot of fun. Later, they felt hungry so they went to a café and they had sandwiches and a salad for lunch.

Test 3

Writing Part 6

Question 31

> Hi Jacob,
> I'd really like to join the chess club. When do the members of the club meet? How often do they play chess at the club? I've never played chess before.

Writing Part 7

Question 32

In the morning, Johnny was is unhappy because his sister Rachel was listening to music and singing loudly. In the afternoon, Rachel was angry because Johnny was talking loudly on his phone. At night, they played video games together and had fun.

Test 4

Writing Part 6

Question 31

> Hi Alex,
> What time do you want to meet on Saturday? I can come to your house at 4 p.m. I'm going to wear my blue trousers and a blue and purple top. I'm going to bring some snacks and bottles of lemonade to the party.

Writing Part 7

Question 32

Yesterday, the teacher told the class about a school project. In the afternoon, Ben looked for information on the subject in the library. This morning, Ben spoke about the subject in front of the class. He was nervous, but everybody liked it.

Test 5

Writing Part 6

Question 31

> Hi Lily,
> I bought a camera online, but it doesn't work. I don't think there's a problem with the battery because it works in my old camera. What should I do?

Writing Part 7

Question 32

Anna saw a poster for a music competition at school. She practised the keyboard at home. During the competition, she played the keyboard on a stage. There were lots of people in the audience. She played really well and she won the competition.

Test 6

Writing Part 6

Question 31

> Hi Ethan,
> When does your flight arrive? What food do you like? Is there any food you don't like? Mum wants to know. There's a rock concert next week we could go to it.

Writing Part 7

Question 32

Last weekend it was my friend's birthday. My sister and I baked a cake for him. We took it to his house to surprise him and we also gave him a present. He was very happy. We ate the cake together and it was delicious.

Test 7

Writing Part 6

Question 31

> Hello Zoe,
> I'd like to tell you about the school study club. In this club we help each other with our homework and we study together for tests. We meet every Tuesday at half past three in the library.

Writing Part 7

Question 32

Last week, I broke my violin, so I took it to a musical instrument shop. The man there repaired it while I waited. On Monday, I played my violin in the school concert. I was very happy.

Test 8

Writing Part 6

Question 31

Hi Neil,
Would you like to spend the weekend at my house? You could come on Saturday morning at about ten. We can go swimming in the morning and play video games later in the afternoon.

Writing Part 7

Question 32

Last month, my family and I moved to a new house. We put our furniture and things in boxes. In the new house, there wasn't any furniture. A few hours later, a van brought our things to the new house.

Model answers for Speaking

The model answers for the Speaking parts of Tests 1–8 are highlighted in grey here. You can listen to these model answers online at: www.collins.co.uk/eltresources

Test 1

Speaking Part 1

06a

Examiner:	Good morning. Can I have your mark sheets, please? I'm Hannah Jones. And this is Keith Mantell. What's your name, Candidate A?
Candidate A:	My name's Alicia Perez.
Examiner:	And what's your name, Candidate B?
Candidate B:	My name's Wei Zhang.
Examiner:	Candidate B, how old are you?
Candidate B:	I'm fourteen years old.
Examiner:	Where do you come from, Candidate B?
Candidate B:	I'm from Shanghai in China.
Examiner:	Thank you. Candidate A, how old are you?
Candidate A:	I'm thirteen.
Examiner:	Where do you come from?
Candidate A:	I come from Valencia in Spain.
Examiner:	Thank you. Now, let's talk about sport. Candidate A, what sports do you like?
Candidate A:	I like playing hockey very much. I also enjoy tennis, but I don't play it. I just watch it on TV.
Examiner:	How often do you do sport?
Candidate A:	I play hockey twice a week after school and I have a PE lesson three times a week.
Examiner:	Candidate B, what kind of sports do you do?
Candidate B:	I play volleyball and sometimes I go swimming.
Examiner:	Where do you do sports, Candidate B?
Candidate B:	I play volleyball at the sports centre near my house and I also play in the park with my friends. I go swimming at the sports centre.
Examiner:	Now Candidate A, please tell me something about a sport that you don't like.
Candidate A:	I don't really like sports like skateboarding because they're too dangerous. And I don't like golf. I think it's boring.
Examiner:	Now, let's talk about clothes. Candidate B, what kind of clothes do you usually wear?
Candidate B:	I wear my school uniform during the week. At the weekend, I usually wear jeans and a T-shirt.
Examiner:	How often do you buy new clothes, Candidate B?
Candidate B:	I buy new clothes once every few months because it isn't good for the environment to buy clothes more often.
Examiner:	Candidate A, where do you like shopping for clothes?
Candidate A:	I go to the big department stores in the city centre because I can find anything I want there.
Examiner:	What are your favourite clothes?
Candidate A:	I like following fashions and I wear clothes that I see in magazines.

Examiner:	Now Candidate B, please tell me something about the kind of clothes you don't like to wear.
Candidate B:	I don't like wearing my school uniform because it's boring and uncomfortable.
Examiner:	Thank you.

Speaking Part 2

07a

Examiner:	Now, in this part of the test you are going to talk together.
	Here are some pictures that show different free-time activities.
	Do you like these different free-time activities? Say why or why not. I'll say that again.
	Do you like these different free-time activities? Say why or why not.
	All right? Now, talk together.
Candidate A:	I don't like most of these free-time activities because I prefer to do activities indoors. I enjoy taking photos, but I don't use a camera. I always use my phone. How about you?
Candidate B:	I like some of these activities. They look interesting and I think they're fun. But I agree with you about photos. I also like taking them.
Candidate A:	Which activity do you like the best?
Candidate B:	I love going camping with my friends, sitting around a fire at night and sleeping in a tent. I don't like all museums, but the ones with dinosaurs are exciting. What other activities do you like?
Candidate A:	I like dancing and listening to music.
Examiner:	Candidate A, do you think going camping is fun?
Candidate A:	No, I don't, because I don't like sleeping outside. It's too noisy and uncomfortable.
Examiner:	Candidate B, do you think going surfing with friends is dangerous?
Candidate B:	Yes, I do, because there are big waves in the sea and maybe there are sharks in the water!
Examiner:	So, Candidate A, which of these free-time activities do you like best?
Candidate A:	I like going to museums and learning about people from the past.
Examiner:	And you, Candidate B, which of these free-time activities do you like doing with your friends?
Candidate B:	I like cycling with my friends. We enjoy riding our bikes through the forest in the countryside. It's relaxing and also good exercise.
Examiner:	Thank you.
	Now, do you prefer doing free-time activities after school or at the weekend, Candidate B?
Candidate B:	I prefer doing activities at the weekend.
Examiner:	Why is that, Candidate B?
Candidate B:	Because I have more time. During the week after school, I have to do my homework, so I don't have a lot of time for free-time activities.
Examiner:	And what about you, Candidate A? Do you prefer doing free-time activities after school or at the weekend?
Candidate A:	I prefer doing activities after school.
Examiner:	Do you prefer being active or relaxing at home, Candidate A?
Candidate A:	I prefer relaxing at home because I can read my favourite books.
Examiner:	And you, Candidate B? Do you prefer being active or relaxing at home?
Candidate B:	I prefer being active.
Examiner:	Why, Candidate B?
Candidate B:	Because I want to stay fit and healthy.
Examiner:	Thank you. That is the end of the test.

Test 2

Speaking Part 1

13a

Examiner:	Good afternoon. Can I have your mark sheets, please? I'm David Dolan. And this is Anne Marshall. What's your name, Candidate A?
Candidate A:	My name's Gabriel Charpentier.
Examiner:	And what's your name, Candidate B?
Candidate B:	My name's Martine Auguste.
Examiner:	Candidate B, how old are you?
Candidate B:	I'm fourteen years old.
Examiner:	And where do you live, Candidate B?
Candidate B:	I live in Vienne, not far from Lyon, here in France.
Examiner:	Thank you. Candidate A, how old are you?
Candidate A:	I'm thirteen.
Examiner:	Where do you live?
Candidate A:	I live in Lyon.
Examiner:	Thank you. Now, let's talk about homework. Candidate A, how often do you get homework each week?
Candidate A:	I usually get homework two or three times a week, and always on a Friday so we can study during the weekend.
Examiner:	For which subject do you do the most homework?
Candidate A:	I usually do the most homework for Maths and French because we have some important exams soon.
Examiner:	Candidate B, why do you think young people usually dislike homework?
Candidate B:	I think most young people are tired after school and they don't want to do more schoolwork. They want to chat with their friends and do interesting activities.
Examiner:	Do you think it's important to do your homework, Candidate B?
Candidate B:	Yes, I do because you can practise what you learnt that day and it helps you to remember information.
Examiner:	Now Candidate A, please tell me something about a homework project you enjoyed.
Candidate A:	I enjoyed a science project I did last month. We had to make a model of a space rocket. It was fun!
Examiner:	Now, let's talk about food. Candidate B, what do you usually have for breakfast?
Candidate B:	I usually have cereal or toast with a glass of orange juice or milk. At the weekend, I sometimes have boiled eggs.
Examiner:	What food do you eat at school, Candidate B?
Candidate B:	At lunchtime, I usually eat a sandwich and a piece of fruit, but sometimes my mum gives me last night's dinner to eat, like soup.
Examiner:	Candidate A, what sweet food do you like to eat?
Candidate A:	I'm not keen on sweet food, but if it's someone's birthday, I eat some cake. I sometimes eat chocolate at the weekend.
Examiner:	What's your favourite food?
Candidate A:	My favourite food is fresh vegetables and fruit. I eat a lot of salads. I also like simple food like omelettes or soup.
Examiner:	Now Candidate B, please tell me something about the kind of food you don't like to eat.

Candidate B: I'm not keen on meat, so I don't eat it often. I'm also not a big fan of fish or mushrooms.

Speaking Part 2

🎧 14a

Examiner: Now, in this part of the test you are going to talk together.
Here are some pictures that show different types of holiday.
Do you like these different types of holiday? Say why or why not. I'll say that again.
Do you like these different types of holiday? Say why or why not.
All right? Now, talk together.

Candidate A: I think it's fun to go camping and I enjoy adventure holidays. How about you?

Candidate B: I like camping, too, but I prefer beach holidays or city breaks.

Candidate A: Why do you like beach holidays?

Candidate B: If I'm on holiday in a hot country, then I like beach holidays because you can swim in the sea and play games on the sand with your friends or family. I'm a fan of water sports so when I'm at the beach, I can also go surfing. Why do you like adventure holidays?

Candidate A: Well, I don't like holidays where you sit all day and do nothing. I like to be active on holiday and there are lots of interesting activities to do on adventure holidays. You can climb mountains, do bungee jumping, go rafting …

Candidate B: I agree.

Examiner: Candidate A, why do you enjoy camping?

Candidate A: Because I love sleeping in a tent and cooking food over a fire. We're active during the day and at night we tell stories and sing songs. It's fun.

Examiner: Candidate B, why do you enjoy city breaks?

Candidate B: I like learning about new places and seeing how people live in other countries. Cities are fun places because there are always lots of activities to do and places to see, like museums, theatres and parks.

Examiner: So Candidate A, which of these holidays do you like the best?

Candidate A: If I have to choose between a camping holiday and an adventure holiday, I'll choose a camping holiday because I enjoy nature and exploring the countryside.

Examiner: And you, Candidate B, which of these holidays do you like the best?

Candidate B: I like beach holidays the best. A city break is fun, but you get tired walking around all day and cities are always very busy with lots of people. On a beach, you can enjoy being outdoors but you don't have to be active if you don't want to. It's a great place to relax.

Examiner: Thank you.
Now, would you prefer to go on holiday with your family or friends, Candidate B?

Candidate B: I think I'd prefer to go on holiday with my friends.

Examiner: Why, Candidate B?

Candidate B: Because when you're with your friends, you can chat to someone with the same interests as you. At my school, we go on two school trips every year and it's always lots of fun. We laugh, play games and chat all day.

Examiner: And what about you, Candidate A? Would you prefer to go on holiday with your family or friends?

Candidate A: I'd prefer to go on holiday with my family.

Examiner: Why?

Candidate A: Well, I've got two older brothers and they're at university, so I don't see them often. When they come on holiday with me and my parents, we have a lot of fun together.

Examiner: Do you prefer holidays in your country or holidays in other countries, Candidate A?

Candidate A: I've never been to another country! But I think I prefer holidays in my country. There are lots of great places to see, and I haven't seen them all.

Examiner:	And you, Candidate B? Do you prefer holidays in your country or holidays in other countries?
Candidate B:	I like holidays everywhere! There are lots of interesting things to do in my country, but it's also fun to go to different places.
Examiner:	Thank you. That is the end of the test.

Test 3

Speaking Part 1

20a

Examiner:	Good evening.
	Can I have your mark sheets, please?
	I'm Elizabeth Johnson. And this is Tom Clarke.
	What's your name, Candidate A?
Candidate A:	My name's Kostas Vassilatou.
Examiner:	And what's your name, Candidate B?
Candidate B:	My name's Lisa Puccini.
Examiner:	Candidate B, how old are you?
Candidate B:	I'm fourteen years old.
Examiner:	Where do you come from, Candidate B?
Candidate B:	I'm from Turin in Italy.
Examiner:	Thank you.
	Candidate A, how old are you?
Candidate A:	I'm thirteen.
Examiner:	Where do you come from?
Candidate A:	I come from Patras in Greece.
Examiner:	Thank you.
	Now, let's talk about future plans.
	Candidate A, what are your plans for the weekend?
Candidate A:	On Saturday, it's my birthday so I'm going to go to a concert in the evening. We're going to see our favourite band. I'm really excited!
Examiner:	What are you going to do on Sunday?
Candidate A:	I'm going to play football. My team has an important match in the afternoon.
Examiner:	Candidate B, what plans do you have for next summer?
Candidate B:	I'm going to go to Paris to visit my cousins. They live near there and they are going to show me around the city. I've never been before so I'm very excited.
Examiner:	Would you like to travel when you are older, Candidate B?
Candidate B:	Yes, I would. I'd like to visit different countries around the world. I like learning about new people and places.
Examiner:	Now Candidate A, please tell me something about what you would like to study in the future.
Candidate A:	I'm quite good at science and in the future I'd like to go to university to become a doctor.
Examiner:	Now, let's talk about friends.
	Candidate B, how often do you see your friends?
Candidate B:	I see them every day after school when we walk home together, and I also usually see them at the weekend.
Examiner:	What do you like doing with your friends, Candidate B?
Candidate B:	I'm in a band with two of my friends so we meet at each other's houses and practise playing our instruments. I play the guitar, my best friend plays the drums and my other friend plays the keyboard and sings.
Examiner:	Candidate A, where do your friends live?

Candidate A:	Many of my friends live in the same part of town as me and a few live near the city centre.
Examiner:	When do you see your friends?
Candidate A:	I usually don't see my friends after school because I'm very busy. I have to do my homework and I'm also in a basketball team, so I usually see my friends at the weekend.
Examiner:	Now Candidate B, please tell me something about one of your friends.
Candidate B:	My best friend is Roberto. He's at the same school as me but we aren't in the same class. He enjoys skateboarding and he's won lots of competitions. Once he was in a TV show about skateboarding in my local area.
Examiner:	Thank you.

Speaking Part 2

🎧 21a

Examiner:	Now, in this part of the test you are going to talk together. Here are some pictures that show different types of exercise. Do you like these different types of exercise? Say why or why not. I'll say that again. Do you like these different types of exercise? Say why or why not. All right? Now, talk together.
Candidate A:	I'm quite active and I like exercising, so I think it's fun to go running and swimming. How about you?
Candidate B:	I like swimming, too, but I also like dancing.
Candidate A:	Really? Why do you like dancing?
Candidate B:	I like it because you can dance in any way you like. In many types of dancing, there aren't any rules. You dance to the music you hear, so you're free to be creative. Dancing makes me feel happy and it's great exercise. Why do you like swimming?
Candidate A:	Well, I've always liked it. I enjoy being in the water and I think swimming is really good for your health. Some exercises only help some parts of your body, like your legs in cycling, but when you swim you exercise all your body. I think it's a fantastic way to keep fit.
Examiner:	So, Candidate A, why do you like running?
Candidate A:	Because it's great for your health but it also makes me feel good. I can run when I like and where I like, and I don't need any special equipment to do it.
Examiner:	Candidate B, do you think going to the gym is a fun way to exercise?
Candidate B:	No, I don't. I think going to the gym is boring and I don't like using the equipment there. I tried going to a gym a year ago, but there were always lots of people and it was too busy.
Examiner:	So Candidate A, which of these types of exercise do you do most often?
Candidate A:	I go running most often. I usually go running with my dad after school, once or twice a week. Then on Sunday morning, I go running with a friend from school.
Examiner:	And you, Candidate B, which of these types of exercise do you do most often?
Candidate B:	I go to dance practice three times a week, on Mondays, Tuesdays and Fridays. I sometimes go swimming at the weekend but not as often as dancing because dancing is also my hobby.
Examiner:	Thank you.
Examiner:	Now, do you prefer exercising in the week or at the weekend, Candidate B?
Candidate B:	I prefer exercising in the week.
Examiner:	Why, Candidate B?
Candidate B:	Well, I have dance practice in the week, but I also prefer it because it's a nice way to relax and think of something else after school. At the weekend, I don't like getting up early to exercise. I prefer to relax.

Examiner:	And what about you, Candidate A? Do you prefer exercising in the week or at the weekend?
Candidate A:	I prefer exercising at the weekend. But I know it's good to exercise during the week as well.
Examiner:	Do you prefer exercising with friends or on your own, Candidate A?
Candidate A:	I prefer exercising with friends – or with my dad. You can chat while you're exercising and you don't get lonely.
Examiner:	And you, Candidate B? Do you prefer exercising with friends or on your own?
Candidate B:	I prefer exercising with friends or with a team.
Examiner:	Why is that, Candidate B?
Candidate B:	Because it's more fun to be with others, and you can learn from others and improve your own skills.
Examiner:	Thank you. That is the end of the test.

Test 4

Speaking Part 1

27a

Examiner:	Good morning.
	Can I have your mark sheets, please?
	I'm Barry Alderton and this is Tricia Parker.
	What's your name, Candidate A?
Candidate A:	My name's Alejandro Romero.
Examiner:	And what's your name, Candidate B?
Candidate B:	My name's Maria Perez.
Examiner:	Candidate B, how old are you?
Candidate B:	I'm fourteen years old.
Examiner:	Where do you live, Candidate B?
Candidate B:	I live here, in Madrid.
Examiner:	Thank you.
	Candidate A, how old are you?
Candidate A:	I'm thirteen.
Examiner:	Where do you live?
Candidate A:	I live in Madrid too, but I come from Segovia.
Examiner:	Thank you.
	Now, let's talk about family.
	Candidate A, what do you enjoy doing with your family?
Candidate A:	I enjoy baking cakes with my grandmother and also going for walks in the forest with my parents and brother.
Examiner:	What do you like about baking?
Candidate A:	My grandmother is the best at baking cakes and biscuits and she's also fun to be with. I learn lots of traditional recipes from her.
Examiner:	Candidate B, what do you like to do at the weekend with your family?
Candidate B:	My family and I have a yearly ticket for my local football club, so we watch matches at the stadium. We like cheering on our team with the other fans!
Examiner:	What do you like to eat when you go out with your family, Candidate B?
Candidate B:	Well, we don't often eat out – it's quite expensive where we live, but when we do, we like Italian food, so we go for pizza.
Examiner:	Now Candidate A, please tell me about something interesting that you did with your family recently.
Candidate A:	Last weekend, we went to an old car show. We saw lots of old cars from the past, and some were nearly 100 years old! My dad and I are fans of old cars, so we really enjoyed it.
Examiner:	Now, let's talk about holidays.

	Candidate B, did you do anything interesting on your holiday?
Candidate B:	Yes, we did. My family and I went to Rome on a city break. It was amazing! But there were lots of people there and the streets were crowded.
Examiner:	What do you like doing on holiday, Candidate B?
Candidate B:	I'm really into art so I like going to art galleries and museums to look at old and new art. That's why it was great in Rome because I saw art from hundreds of years ago!
Examiner:	Candidate A, how often do you go on holiday?
Candidate A:	My family and I go maybe two or three times a year.
Examiner:	When do you go on holiday, Candidate A?
Candidate A:	We go for a few weeks during the school summer holidays in August, and then sometimes during the holidays in April and December.
Examiner:	Now Candidate B, please tell me something about a place that you enjoyed visiting.
Candidate B:	Last year, we visited Cornwall in the UK. I really enjoyed seeing the small villages and towns there. I also had surfing lessons and that was really cool!

Speaking Part 2

28a

Examiner:	Now, in this part of the test you are going to talk together.
	Here are some pictures that show different types of entertainment.
	Do you like these different types of entertainment? Say why or why not. I'll say that again.
	Do you like these different types of entertainment? Say why or why not.
	All right? Now, talk together.
Candidate A:	I think playing video games and chess is fun. How about you?
Candidate B:	I like playing video games, too, but I think going to music festivals is more fun.
Candidate A:	Why do you think festivals are more fun?
Candidate B:	Because you can listen to your favourite band or singer and you're with all the other fans, and the atmosphere is fantastic. I like listening to music on my laptop, but it's more exciting when you hear it live at a festival. I also like to dance there, and you don't have to listen to the music with headphones, like at home! What do you like about video games?
Candidate A:	Well, I like adventure games where you have to solve a puzzle – they really make you think. I also like playing video games with my friends because it's a fun way to relax.
Examiner:	Candidate A, why do you think playing chess is fun?
Candidate A:	Because you have to think a lot and it takes lots of skill to win a game of chess. And I love winning!
Examiner:	Candidate B, do you think playing board games is interesting?
Candidate B:	Not really. I find most board games boring. I only play them if it's a rainy day and I can't go outside. I prefer to be active.
Examiner:	So Candidate A, which of these types of entertainment do you like the best?
Candidate A:	I like playing chess the best. It isn't only a fun game; it's also good for your brain because you have to think about your next move and how to win.
Examiner:	And you, Candidate B, which of these types of entertainment do you like the best?
Candidate B:	I like music concerts or festivals the best because you can make new friends and listen to your favourite music. But I also enjoy watching some TV programmes with my friends and family, especially comedies!
Examiner:	Thank you.
	Now, do you prefer enjoying yourself indoors or outside, Candidate B?
Candidate B:	I prefer having fun outside.
Examiner:	Why, Candidate B?
Candidate B:	Because you can be more active outside and I think you can find more things to do.

Examiner:	And what about you, Candidate A? Do you prefer enjoying yourself indoors or outside?
Candidate A:	I prefer having fun indoors because, for example, you can play games in all kinds of weather. If it rains, you don't need to stop playing.
Examiner:	Do you prefer having fun with friends or family, Candidate A?
Candidate A:	I prefer having fun with my family. My brother enjoys playing chess as well, so we often play with each other – and I usually win!
Examiner:	And you, Candidate B? Do you prefer having fun with friends or family?
Candidate B:	I like having fun with my friends *and* my family.
Examiner:	Why, Candidate B?
Candidate B:	I love my family and we always have fun, even sitting and talking. And I love having fun with my friends because we have the same hobbies and we like doing the same things.
Examiner:	Thank you. That is the end of the test.

Test 5

Speaking Part 1

🎧 34a

Examiner:	Good afternoon.
	Can I have your mark sheets, please?
	I'm Angela Burrows and this is Bob Jenkins.
	What's your name, Candidate A?
Candidate A:	My name's Julia Schmidt.
Examiner:	And what's your name, Candidate B?
Candidate B:	My name's Francisco Ronaldo.
Examiner:	Candidate B, how old are you?
Candidate B:	I'm fourteen years old.
Examiner:	Where do you come from, Candidate B?
Candidate B:	I'm from Coimbra in Portugal.
Examiner:	Thank you.
	Candidate A, how old are you?
Candidate A:	I'm thirteen.
Examiner:	Where do you come from?
Candidate A:	I come from Vienna in Austria.
Examiner:	Thank you.
	Now, let's talk about places in a town.
	Candidate A, which places in your town are popular with young people?
Candidate A:	The parks are popular, and there's also a square in my neighbourhood where a lot of young people go. I like to meet my friends there at the weekend.
Examiner:	Why do you like it there?
Candidate A:	Because there are some great cafés where we can buy hot chocolate or juice and we can sit and talk.
Examiner:	Candidate B, what places are popular with young people?
Candidate B:	Places like cinemas, parks and sports centres. You can have fun there and they're good places to meet your friends.
Examiner:	What places would you like in your neighbourhood that you don't have, Candidate B?
Candidate B:	I'd like to have a skate park and maybe a bowling alley.
Examiner:	Now Candidate A, please tell me something about a place you go to when you want to relax.
Candidate A:	I'm lucky because there are some lovely parks in my city, so when I want to relax, I go there with my friends for a picnic.
Examiner:	Now, let's talk about shopping.
	Candidate B, how often do you go shopping?

Candidate B:	I usually go shopping once a week on Saturday with my friends, and I sometimes go to the supermarket with my parents during the week.
Examiner:	When do you buy new clothes, Candidate B?
Candidate B:	I don't buy new clothes often because it's better to wear your clothes as long as possible. I go shopping two or three times a year with my mum or dad if I need clothes for school, but if I need jeans or T-shirts, I go with my friends.
Examiner:	Candidate A, where do you usually go shopping?
Candidate A:	I usually go shopping at department stores, or I go to local shops.
Examiner:	Who do you usually go shopping with?
Candidate A:	I usually go shopping to the supermarket with my mum or dad, but I sometimes go shopping with my friends at the weekend.
Examiner:	Now Candidate B, please tell me about something you bought recently.
Candidate B:	On Saturday I bought a book from my favourite bookshop near my house – it's by my favourite author.

Speaking Part 2

🎧
35a

Examiner:	Now, in this part of the test you are going to talk together. Here are some pictures that show different types of homes. Do you like these different types of homes? Say why or why not. I'll say that again. Do you like these different types of homes? Say why or why not. All right? Now, talk together.
Candidate A:	I think it would be fun to live on a houseboat or on a farm. How about you?
Candidate B:	I don't think I'd like to live in a farmhouse on a farm. Farmers have a very hard job. But I'd like the small wooden house in the mountains – for a holiday.
Candidate A:	Why do you like the house in the mountains?
Candidate B:	It's beautiful, and I'd love to stay there for a few weeks in the winter. When it snows, you can light a fire and the house will be warm and cosy. Also, I love snowboarding, so it would be great to be in the mountains. Why would you like to live in the farmhouse?
Candidate A:	Well, I love animals, and if you live on a farm, you can keep different types of animals, like horses and donkeys. Also, a farmhouse is in the countryside, and I love being close to nature.
Examiner:	Candidate A, why do you think living on a houseboat is fun?
Candidate A:	Because it's boring to live in one place all the time. If you live on a houseboat, you can travel to different places whenever you like.
Examiner:	Candidate B, would you like to live in an apartment building like this?
Candidate B:	No, I wouldn't. I don't like living very high up and you don't have a garden if you live in a flat. It's also noisy because you have other people living very close to you.
Examiner:	So Candidate A, which of these homes do you like the best?
Candidate A:	Well, if I have to choose between a houseboat and a farmhouse, I will choose the houseboat because I think it's less work than living on a farm. It's hard work looking after animals all the time – although I love animals.
Examiner:	And you, Candidate B, which of these homes do you like the best?
Candidate B:	I like the house in the mountains the best. You can enjoy being outdoors and you live in a really interesting home. You can walk in the forest and see birds and other wild animals.
Examiner:	Thank you. Now, would you prefer to live in a big home or a small home, Candidate B?
Candidate B:	I'd prefer to live in a big home.
Examiner:	Why, Candidate B?

Candidate B:	Because you have space for all your things. My family and I live in a flat, but if we lived in a big house with a garden we could sit outside when the weather is good. And we could have barbecues every weekend and invite all our friends.
Examiner:	And what about you, Candidate A? Would you prefer to live in a big home or a small home?
Candidate A:	I'm not sure, but I think I'd prefer a small home.
Examiner:	Would you prefer to live in a city or in the countryside?
Candidate A:	I'm not sure. I love the country, and I love nature, but in the city you have everything you need there – shops, parks, restaurants, sports centres, cinemas, everything.
Examiner:	And you, Candidate B? Would you prefer to live in a city or in the countryside?
Candidate B:	I'd prefer to live in the countryside.
Examiner:	Why is that, Candidate B?
Candidate B:	Because it's quieter than a city, and you can go for long walks with your family and enjoy nature.
Examiner:	Thank you. That is the end of the test.

Test 6

Speaking Part 1

🎧 41a

Examiner:	Good evening. Can I have your mark sheets, please? I'm William Stone. And this is Caroline Morris. What's your name, Candidate A?
Candidate A:	My name's Sakura Ito.
Examiner:	And what's your name, Candidate B?
Candidate B:	My name's Shiro Yamada.
Examiner:	Candidate B, how old are you?
Candidate B:	I'm fourteen years old.
Examiner:	Where do you live, Candidate B?
Candidate B:	I live in Kyoto, in Japan.
Examiner:	Thank you. Candidate A, how old are you?
Candidate A:	I'm thirteen.
Examiner:	Where do you live?
Candidate A:	I also live in Kyoto.
Examiner:	Thank you.
Examiner:	Now, let's talk about favourite subjects. Candidate A, what is your favourite subject at school?
Candidate A:	My favourite subject is geography because I love learning about people and places around the world.
Examiner:	What do you want to study in the future?
Candidate A:	I want to go to university and get a diploma in farm management. My grandparents have a small farm and I want to look after it one day.
Examiner:	Candidate B, what subjects do you enjoy at school?
Candidate B:	I enjoy maths and Science because they are the most interesting subjects. I'd like to earn a good salary in the future and work as an engineer, so it's important to be good in these subjects.
Examiner:	Would you like to study in Japan or would you like to study in another country, Candidate B?
Candidate B:	I'd prefer to study in Japan and be near my family.
Examiner:	Now Candidate A, please tell me something about a subject that you don't enjoy at school.

Candidate A:	I don't really enjoy art because I'm not good at drawing and painting, It's a bit boring as well.
Examiner:	Now, let's talk about television. Candidate B, how often do you watch television?
Candidate B:	I'm busy during the week and I have to study for school in the evenings, so I don't watch TV often. I sometimes watch it at the weekend.
Examiner:	What kind of television programmes do you watch, Candidate B?
Candidate B:	I enjoy watching sport like baseball and tennis, and I also like programmes about animals and nature.
Examiner:	Candidate A, do you watch a lot of television?
Candidate A:	No, I don't. I sometimes watch sport at the weekend, or a film, and I also like comedies and quiz shows.
Examiner:	Who do you watch TV with, Candidate A?
Candidate A:	My brother and I watch sport together, and Dad enjoys watching a good film with us too. But I watch quiz shows on my own.
Examiner:	Now Candidate B, please tell me about the sort of television programmes that you don't like.
Candidate B:	I don't like watching the news, and soap operas are boring. I also hate programmes where people talk about themselves all the time.

Speaking Part 2

🎧
42a

Examiner:	Now, in this part of the test you are going to talk together. Here are some pictures that show different ways to travel. Do you like these different ways to travel? Say why or why not. I'll say that again. Do you like these different ways to travel? Say why or why not. All right? Now, talk together.
Candidate A:	I think it's nice to travel by boat and by bike. What do you think?
Candidate B:	I like travelling by boat, too, because I love the water, but I also like trains.
Candidate A:	Why do you like to travel by train?
Candidate B:	Because you can get to different places fast. It's faster than walking or going by bus. I like looking out of the window while I am travelling and I can see the different places we pass. Why do you like travelling by boat?
Candidate A:	I think it's fun to be on a boat in the sea. It isn't the best way to travel if you want to go somewhere fast, but you can relax. If you want to go to another country, the best way is by plane.
Examiner:	Candidate A, why do you think it is nice to travel by bike?
Candidate A:	Because it's good for your health and it's also good for the environment.
Examiner:	Candidate B, do you think travelling by plane is exciting?
Candidate B:	No, I don't, not anymore. When I was younger, I liked travelling by plane because I liked looking out of the window, but now I think it's tiring and boring to be on a plane for a long time.
Examiner:	Now, Candidate A, which of these ways to travel do you like the best?
Candidate A:	Well, I will choose travelling by bike because it's better for the world around us, and it's also a good way to keep fit and see different places. But you can't travel everywhere by bike, and sometimes you need to travel by boat, too.
Examiner:	And you, Candidate B, which of these ways to travel do you like the best?
Candidate B:	I like trains the best. We've got great trains in Japan, and they go really fast. I can travel from city to city, or to any place that I like. I like chatting with other people while we travel, too.
Examiner:	Thank you. Now, do you prefer travelling on your own or with friends, Candidate B?

Candidate B:	I prefer travelling with other people, but I can't always do that.
Examiner:	Why do you like travelling with other people, Candidate B?
Candidate B:	Because it's more fun and I don't get bored. When I go to school on the bus, I am usually on my own, and I don't like that.
Examiner:	And what about you, Candidate A? Do you prefer travelling on your own or with friends?
Candidate A:	I prefer travelling on my own because I can think.
Examiner:	Do you prefer travelling by bus or by car, Candidate A?
Candidate A:	I prefer travelling by car because you can start your journey any time you want, go where you want to go, and you don't need to stop at bus stops.
Examiner:	And you, Candidate B? Do you prefer travelling by bus or by car?
Candidate B:	I prefer travelling by bus.
Examiner:	Why, Candidate B?
Candidate B:	Because it passes lots of interesting places. I also think it's better for the environment.
Examiner:	Thank you. That is the end of the test.

Test 7

Speaking Part 1

🎧 48a

Examiner:	Good morning. Can I have your mark sheets, please? I'm Monica Taylor. And this is Sam Chapman. What's your name, Candidate A?
Candidate A:	My name's Jose Fernandes.
Examiner:	And what's your name, Candidate B?
Candidate B:	My name's Sofie Larsen.
Examiner:	Candidate B, how old are you?
Candidate B:	I'm fourteen years old.
Examiner:	Where do you come from, Candidate B?
Candidate B:	I'm from Bergen in Norway.
Examiner:	Thank you. Candidate A, how old are you?
Candidate A:	I'm thirteen.
Examiner:	Where do you come from?
Candidate A:	I come from Rio de Janeiro in Brazil.
Examiner:	Thank you. Now, let's talk about hobbies. Candidate A, what hobbies do you have?
Candidate A:	I like drawing and I'm a big fan of Japanese art, so I like drawing manga-style cartoons in my spare time.
Examiner:	Why do you like drawing?
Candidate A:	Because it's great to make something new. I like using my imagination. It also helps me to relax and forget about things that worry me, like my schoolwork.
Examiner:	Candidate B, what kinds of hobbies are popular with your friends?
Candidate B:	My friends all have different kinds of hobbies. One of my friends likes doing sport, another friend plays the guitar and my best friend is really into photography.
Examiner:	What hobbies would you like to try, Candidate B?
Candidate B:	I'd like to try horse riding. I've never ridden a horse before. I think it would be really exciting!
Examiner:	Now Candidate A, please tell me something about a hobby you wouldn't like to try.

Candidate A:	Well, I wouldn't like to dance or sing. I'm a shy person and I don't like performing in front of other people.
Examiner:	Now, let's talk about jobs. Candidate B, what kind of weekend jobs are popular with young people?
Candidate B:	I think working as a shop assistant or a waiter is popular with young people.
Examiner:	What job would you like to do, Candidate B?
Candidate B:	When I leave school, I'd like to go to university to study medicine. I want to be a doctor in the future.
Examiner:	Candidate A, would you like to have your own business in the future?
Candidate A:	Yes, I think so because it would be nice to be a boss, but it's also lots of hard work.
Examiner:	What type of business would you have?
Candidate A:	I think I'd like a photography business. I'm quite good at taking photos with my camera, so I could take photos of people at different special events.
Examiner:	Now Candidate B, please tell me something about a job you wouldn't want to do.
Candidate B:	I wouldn't like to work in a dentist's surgery. I'm scared of the dentist, and I don't like the noise of all the different equipment.

Speaking Part 2

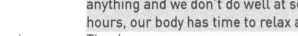

Examiner:	Now, in this part of the test you are going to talk together. Here are some pictures that show different ways to stay healthy. Do you like these different ways to stay healthy? Say why or why not. I'll say that again. Do you like these different ways to stay healthy? Say why or why not. All right? Now, talk together.
Candidate A:	I think it's very important to exercise often, eat fresh food and drink lots of water. How about you?
Candidate B:	I agree that exercising is important, and healthy food is good for us, but lots of sleep is also important.
Candidate A:	Why do you think sleep is so important?
Candidate B:	Well, when you go to bed early you feel better in the morning. A good night's sleep helps you to learn better at school the next day. If I stay up late and don't get enough sleep, I find it difficult to listen to my teacher at school. Why do you think exercising often is good for you?
Candidate A:	I think it's good for us because it helps us not to get ill very often. It helps us relax and it makes our body stronger. When I have lots of homework or when I'm studying for exams, I take regular breaks and do some exercise. It helps me think and remember better.
Examiner:	Candidate A, how do you think reading helps you keep healthy?
Candidate A:	Because it helps you relax. It's much better for you than watching TV or playing video games, which are bad for you if you look at a screen for many hours.
Examiner:	Candidate B, do you think walking is good for you?
Candidate B:	Yes, I do, but you have to walk quickly or for a long time. If you walk slowly, I don't think it helps you stay healthy.
Examiner:	So Candidate A, which of these ways to stay healthy do you think is the best?
Candidate A:	I think that exercising is the best way to stay healthy because it's good for your body and your mind. You stay strong and you don't get so tired.
Examiner:	And you, Candidate B, which of these ways to stay healthy do you think is the best?
Candidate B:	I think getting lots of sleep is the best. When we're tired, we feel like we can't do anything and we don't do well at school. But if we sleep for the correct number of hours, our body has time to relax and we feel good in the morning.
Examiner:	Thank you.

Examiner:	Now, Candidate B, what kind of food do you think is good for you?
Candidate B:	I think vegetables and fruit are very important. And things like milk and yoghurt and fish.
Examiner:	Which ones do you like, Candidate B?
Candidate B:	I like vegetables and I usually eat them at lunch and dinner, but I also eat fruit as a snack during the day.
Examiner:	And what about you, Candidate A? What kind of food do you think is good for you?
Candidate A:	Fruit, vegetables, fish, milk, cheese, and not a lot of meat. I eat lots of fruit every day.
Examiner:	Which fruit do you like, Candidate A?
Candidate A:	I like all fruit, but I don't like many vegetables. The only vegetables I like are peas and tomatoes.
Examiner:	Do you like waking up early or late, Candidate A?
Candidate A:	I prefer waking up late because I usually chat to my friends late at night. So it's difficult to wake up early in the mornings.
Examiner:	And you, Candidate B? Do you like waking up early or late?
Candidate B:	I like waking up early.
Examiner:	Why is that, Candidate B?
Candidate B:	Because I have lots of time to do the things I need to do. I usually go to bed quite early, too, so it's easier to wake up in the morning.
Examiner:	Thank you. That is the end of the test.

Test 8

Speaking Part 1

55a

Examiner:	Good afternoon.
	Can I have your mark sheets, please?
	I'm James Bennett. And this is Ursula Brown.
	What's your name, Candidate A?
Candidate A:	My name's Andrea Koch.
Examiner:	And what's your name, Candidate B?
Candidate B:	My name's David Luschin.
Examiner:	Candidate B, how old are you?
Candidate B:	I'm fourteen years old.
Examiner:	Where do you live, Candidate B?
Candidate B:	I live in Vienna.
Examiner:	Thank you.
	Candidate A, how old are you?
Candidate A:	I'm thirteen.
Examiner:	Where do you live?
Candidate A:	I live in Villach.
Examiner:	Thank you.
	Now, let's talk about music.
	Candidate A, what is your favourite type of music?
Candidate A:	I'm a big fan of rock music. I often listen to rock on my phone on the way to school.
Examiner:	Why do you like rock?
Candidate A:	Because it has a good rhythm. Rock music is exciting; it never sounds boring.
Examiner:	Candidate B, what kind of music do your friends listen to?
Candidate B:	They listen to all kinds of music – pop, hip hop, dance music and classical music.
Examiner:	What kind of music do you often listen to, Candidate B?
Candidate B:	I listen to all kinds of music on the radio or online. Sometimes I enjoy classical music if I want to relax and I listen to pop music if I want to dance.
Examiner:	Now Candidate A, please tell me something about music that you don't like.
Candidate A:	I'm not a big fan of hip hop because I think they talk or sing too fast, and most of the time it just sounds like shouting to me.

Examiner:	Now, let's talk about your home. Candidate B, what is your favourite room in your home?
Candidate B:	Well, my favourite room is my bedroom. I spend most of my time there after school.
Examiner:	What do you like best about your bedroom, Candidate B?
Candidate B:	My bedroom is not very big, but it has enough space. I have an armchair opposite the window so I can look outside and see the view. It's really comfortable. I have a big bed, too.
Examiner:	Candidate A, where do you and your family spend most of your time at home?
Candidate A:	In the evenings, we often spend our time in the living room. We read books, watch TV and sometimes play board games together.
Examiner:	What is your bedroom like, Candidate A?
Candidate A:	It's quite big and it has a wardrobe for my clothes. My desk is in front of the window so it's nice and light while I'm doing my homework. I've got lots of posters on the wall, too.
Examiner:	Now Candidate B, please tell me about something you don't like about your home.
Candidate B:	My home is near a busy road. I live in an apartment in the city centre and it is often noisy outside.

Speaking Part 2

56a

Examiner:	Now, in this part of the test you are going to talk together. Here are some pictures that show different types of weather. Do you like these different types of weather? Say why or why not. I'll say that again. Do you like these different types of weather? Say why or why not. All right? Now, talk together.
Candidate A:	I like it when it's hot and sunny because then you can sit outside and enjoy trees and flowers. But it's also exciting when there's a thunderstorm. What type of weather do you like?
Candidate B:	I don't really like hot weather, especially in the town. I prefer it when it's cool and windy.
Candidate A:	Why do you like cool and windy weather?
Candidate B:	I like being in the countryside and walking in the mountains. It's easier to walk when the weather is cool because you don't get too hot. It's difficult to walk when you get hot and sweaty. Why do you like thunderstorms?
Candidate A:	I think it's fun to watch them from my bedroom window. I like to see all the bright flashes from the lightning and hear the loud noise of the thunder.
Examiner:	Candidate A, do you enjoy snowy weather?
Candidate A:	Well, I like to see the snow because it makes everything look very beautiful, but I don't like going out in the snow very much. It's too cold!
Examiner:	Candidate B, how do you feel about rainy weather?
Candidate B:	I love it. I put on a raincoat and go for a walk, but I have to be careful in the city. When cars go past, they often splash me with water.
Examiner:	So Candidate A, which of these types of weather do you like best?
Candidate A:	I like hot sunny weather the best because it makes me feel happy and it makes everything in my city look beautiful. The mountains near Villach are lovely in the summer.
Examiner:	And you, Candidate B, which of these types of weather do you like best?
Candidate B:	I like thunderstorms the best because it's exciting to see the lightning in the sky.
Examiner:	Thank you.
Examiner:	Now, do you prefer the summer or the winter, Candidate B?
Candidate B:	I prefer winter.
Examiner:	Why, Candidate B?

Candidate B:	I'm an active person and I love winter sports. My family and I go skiing in the Tyrol, every winter. I'm not so keen on sport in the summer because, as I said before, I don't like hot weather very much.
Examiner:	And what about you, Candidate A? Do you prefer the summer or the winter?
Candidate A:	I prefer the summer because I love going to the lakes with my friends and swimming or windsurfing.
Examiner:	Do you prefer to visit hot countries or cold countries on holiday, Candidate A?
Candidate A:	I prefer to visit hot countries because you don't need to take lots of clothes with you. You just need T-shirts and shorts, and a pair of sunglasses. And you can go swimming in the sea and surfing!
Examiner:	And you, Candidate B? Do you prefer to visit hot countries or cold countries on holiday?
Candidate B:	I prefer hot countries if they have beaches and I can go swimming in the sea and keep cool.
Examiner:	Thank you. That is the end of the test.

Speaking: Additional practice by topic

This section will give you extra practice in the sorts of questions the examiner may ask you in Part 1 of the Speaking test. Listen to the audio and practise answering the questions. Some of the questions are similar but the words used in the question are different; this gives you more speaking practice and shows you how different questions are formed. Remember that the examiner will choose what questions to ask you and won't ask you lots of questions about the same topic.

When you are practising try to give a longer answer, even if you want to just say *No*. For example, you may not like doing sport, but if the question is *Do you like playing tennis?* and your real answer is *No*, you can say something like *No, I don't like playing tennis because I didn't learn how to play it when I was at school*. Once you are feeling confident it would be a good idea not to look at the book – just listen to the audio and answer the questions. And keep practising!

The questions are grouped under different topic headings: books and films; clothes and accessories; communication and technology; family and friends; food; health and exercise; hobbies and interests; house and home; personal feelings and experiences; places; school; shopping; sport; the natural world and weather; travel and transport; work and jobs.

Books and films

57

Now let's talk about books and films.
Tell us about your favourite book.
Tell us about your favourite film.
Do you have a favourite actor? What is his or her name?
What type of films do you like to watch?
What type of films do you dislike watching?
Do you have cinema near to where you live?
How often do you go to the cinema?
What types of books do you read?
How many books do you read every month?
What types of books do you like?
Do you have a favourite author?
Is there a library at your school? Is there a library where you live?
Do you read books at the library?
How often do you buy books? Where do you buy them?
Do you ever watch films online?
Who do you enjoy watching films with?

Clothes and accessories

58

Now let's talk about clothes and accessories.
Tell us about the clothes and accessories you are wearing today.
What clothes do you usually wear?
Do you like to wear clothes that are in fashion?
What are your favourite clothes?
Where's your favourite place to buy clothes?
Do you have to wear a uniform to school?
Do you spend a lot of money on clothes and accessories?
What accessories do you often wear?
What clothes and accessories must you not wear at school?
Do you look at fashion on social media or the Internet?
What clothes do you wear in the winter?
Can you describe the clothes that you like to wear?
What do teenagers like to wear in your country?
Do you ever wear jewellery?
How were clothes different in the past?
Do you ever have to wear special clothes? What clothes are they? Where do you wear them?

Communication and technology

Now let's talk about communication and technology.
Tell us about what technology you use at school.
Do you have a mobile phone?
Are there many computers at your school?
What technology do you use every day?
What technology do you use at home?
How do you prefer to chat with your friends?
Do you ever send letters by post?
Do you prefer to use a laptop or a computer?
Do you like to talk to friends online?
Who do you like to call on the phone?
How often do you call your friends on the phone?
Do you ever call any of your family on the phone?
How do you listen to music?
Who was the last person you spoke to on the phone?
How often do you send emails?
Have you ever used a digital camera? When?

Family and friends

Now let's talk about family and friends.
Tell us about your family.
Who do you live with?
What do your family members look like?
Do you have any brothers or sisters?
Do you have any grandparents?
What activities do you and your family like to do together?
Can you describe an important person in your family?
What do you do with your family at the weekend?
Tell us about your friends.
Do you live near any of your friends?
How often do you see your friends?
What do you like doing with your friends?
Where do you like to go with your friends?
Do your friends have the same hobbies as you?
Where did you meet your best friend?

Food

Now let's talk about food.
Tell us about your favourite food.
What did you have for lunch yesterday?
What time do you eat breakfast?
What do you usually eat after school?
What time do you have dinner?
Who cooks your meals at home?
Is there any food that you dislike?
How often do you eat at a restaurant?
What do you like to eat with friends?
Do you eat sweets with your friends? What do you eat?
What is your favourite dessert?
What fruit do you like to eat?
What food is popular where you live?
Are there any famous dishes in your country? What are they?
What food do people like to eat when they visit your country?

Health and exercise

Now let's talk about health and exercise.
Tell us about what exercise you like to do.
How often do you exercise every week?
Are there any types of exercise you dislike?
What sport do you play at school?
Do you like to exercise alone or with other people?
When was the last time you were ill?
What do you do when you don't feel well?
Who takes care of you when you don't feel well?
When was the last time you visited the doctors?
Do you like to eat healthy food? What do you eat?
How often do you eat fruit and vegetables?
Do you think it's important to walk often?
What sport do you usually play at the weekend?
Do you do any exercise after school?
What do you do to stay healthy?

Hobbies and interests

Now let's talk about hobbies and interests.
Tell us about your hobbies and interests.
What hobbies do you do?
When do you do them?
Who do you do your hobbies with?
Have you ever been camping with your friends?
What activities do you like to do together?
What do you like to do at the weekend?
Do you like listening to music? What do you listen to?
Who is your favourite band or singer?
What do you like to do after school?
Do you like going to concerts or festivals?
Can you play an instrument? What instrument do you play?
How often do you go to museums?
Did you collect anything when you were younger?
Do you enjoy riding your bike? Where do you go?
What do you like to do on holiday?

House and home

Now let's talk about house and home.
Tell us about the place where you live.
Is your home in a town, in a city or in the countryside?
What is your home like?
Who do you live with?
What rooms do you have in your home?
What does your bedroom look like?
Which is your favourite room in your home?
What furniture do you have in your home?
What jobs do you do at home?
Is your home modern or old?
What do you like about your home?
Is there anything you dislike about your home?
What places are there near your home?
What do you do when you go home after school?
How often do your friends visit you at home?

Personal feelings and experiences
Now let's talk about feelings and experiences.
Tell us about how you feel today.
What things make you happy?
Is there anything that makes you angry?
What makes you feel worried?
Who do you speak to if you feel worried?
Tell us about a time you felt brave.
Tell us about a time you felt tired.
What things make you feel bored?
Tell us about your favourite experience.
Have you ever had a special time in your life?
How do you celebrate your birthday?
What is your favourite time of the year?
Tell us about what you thought of your last holiday.
What do you find interesting?

Places
Now let's talk about places.
Tell us about the place where you live.
Do you prefer to live in a town, in a city or in the countryside? Why?
What is your favourite place in the countryside?
Are there any mountains in your country?
Are there many shops in your town?
Do you live near the sea or beach?
Do you like walking in the countryside?
What buildings are there in your town or city?
What is the best place in your town or city?
Tell us about the countryside near where you live.
Where is the nearest airport?
How far from your home is your school?
Do you live in a busy or quiet place?
What interesting places are there near your home?
What is the most beautiful place near where you live?

School
Now let's talk about school.
Tell us about your school.
How many students are there at your school?
Who is your favourite teacher? Why?
What is your favourite subject?
What do you do during break time at school?
Where do you eat lunch at school?
What do you find difficult at school?
What lessons do you think are the most interesting? Why?
Who do you sit next to in class?
Do you get a lot of homework at school?
When do you have tests at school?
Does your school have a library?
How many years will you stay at your school?
Where would you like to study in the future?
What subjects do you want to learn in the future?

Shopping

68

Now let's talk about shopping.
Tell us about where you usually go shopping.
Do you think shopping is boring or fun? Why?
Who do you often go shopping with?
How often do you go shopping?
What types of shops do you have near your home?
Are there any department stores near your home?
Where do you like to go shopping?
Do you ever go shopping together with your friends?
What do you like to buy?
Who buys your clothes for you?
Who buys the food in your family?
Do you help your family buy the food?
Do you prefer to go shopping alone or with other people?
What things does your family buy every week?
Do you take your own bags when you buy food or do you use plastic bags?

Sport

69

Now let's talk about sport.
Tell us about the sports you like.
What sports do you like to play?
How often do you watch sport on TV?
What sport do you play at school?
When was the last time you went swimming?
Do you ever play sport with your friends?
Is there a sport that you aren't good at?
What sports are you not keen on?
Are you a fan of any sports teams? Which ones?
Which sport is popular in your country?
What sports do you think are interesting?
What sports do you think are fun?
What sports do you think are dangerous?
Have you ever entered a sports competition?
Have you ever won any sports prizes?

The natural world and weather

70

Now let's talk about the natural world and the weather.
Tell us about your favourite season.
What type of weather do you like?
What weather do you often have where you live?
What's the weather like in the winter where you live?
What's the weather like in the summer where you live?
Tell us what nature is like where you live.
How often does it snow where you live?
What activities do you like doing in hot weather?
What activities do you like doing in cold weather?
What types of animals live where you live?
Do you think it's important to take care of nature?
Do you grow any plants or trees where you live?
Where do you enjoy going in your country?
What places do people enjoy visiting in your country?

Travel and transport

Now let's talk about travel and transport.

Tell us about how you travel to school.

What is the best way to travel around where you live?

Is it easy to walk around where you live?

What type of transport is in your town or city?

Do you ever ride your bike where you live? Where do you go?

What transport do you use at the weekend?

What transport do you dislike using?

What is the fastest way to get to school from your home?

Are there a lot of cars near where you live?

Have you ever travelled by train? Where did you go?

Do you like to travel by plane? Why? Why not?

How do you prefer to travel every day?

Do you have many tourists in your country?

How do people who visit your country travel around?

Is the transport good or bad where you live? Why?

Work and jobs

Now let's talk about work and jobs.

Tell us about what you want to do when you leave school.

What type of jobs do you like?

What type of jobs do you dislike?

Would you prefer to work inside or outside?

What jobs do people in your family do?

Does anyone in your family have an interesting job?

What job do you think you would be good at?

What job do you want to do in the future?

What do you need to study to get the job you want?

Is it easy or difficult to get a job where you live?

What job did you want to do when you were younger?

Have you ever had a part-time job?

What clothes did you have to wear at your part-time job?

Do you think it's good to work at the weekend or not?

What do you think is the best job in the world?